Pandemics: A Chronicle of Human Resilience

Oswald D. B.

Published by Oswald, 2024.

While every precaution has been taken in the preparation of this book, the publisher assumes no responsibility for errors or omissions, or for damages resulting from the use of the information contained herein.

PANDEMICS: A CHRONICLE OF HUMAN RESILIENCE

First edition. September 3, 2024.

ISBN: 979-8227150783

Written by Oswald D. B..

Table of Contents

Introduction: The Global Impact of Pandemics

Throughout human history, pandemics have been a profound force, shaping societies, economies, and cultures in ways both visible and invisible. From the Plague of Athens in 430 B.C. to the COVID-19 pandemic that has reshaped our world today, pandemics have repeatedly demonstrated their capacity to disrupt the very fabric of human civilization. They bring with them not just disease and death, but also fear, uncertainty, and often, societal transformation. The story of pandemics is not merely a medical one; it is a story of human resilience, adaptation, and sometimes, profound change.

The Unseen Enemy

Pandemics have a unique and terrifying power: they strike invisibly, moving swiftly across borders and through communities without regard for wealth, power, or geography. Unlike wars or natural disasters, which often have a clear beginning and end, pandemics can linger, leaving a long trail of consequences. The fear they generate can be as deadly as the diseases themselves, leading to social unrest, economic collapse, and political upheaval. Imagine the streets of Athens suddenly deserted, the mighty Roman Empire brought to its knees, or bustling medieval towns turned into ghostly silence—all because of a microscopic foe. These are not just stories from the past; they are vivid reminders of how fragile human societies can be in the face of a pandemic.

Pandemics: More Than Just a Health Crisis

While the immediate concern during a pandemic is health and survival, the ripple effects extend far beyond. Economies crumble as markets crash and industries stall. Cultural practices evolve, sometimes permanently, as communities adapt to new realities. Governments face unprecedented challenges in maintaining order and providing care, often leading to significant shifts in political power. Public health systems are tested to their limits, prompting innovations that can change the course of medical history.

...ics force societies to confront their vulnerabilities, often revealing ...p-seated inequities and driving radical change.

Consider the impact of the Black Death in the 14th century, which killed an estimated 25 million people in Europe alone, wiping out nearly a third of its population. This pandemic didn't just decimate the population—it shattered the existing social order, disrupted economies, and paved the way for profound cultural and religious shifts. Or take the Spanish Flu of 1918, which, in the wake of World War I, spread like wildfire across a weary globe. It claimed more lives than the war itself and exposed the fragility of global public health systems, leading to significant advancements in medical science and public health policy.

Lessons from the Past

History teaches us that while pandemics are inevitable, their outcomes are not preordained. The responses to pandemics—both effective and ineffective—offer a treasure trove of lessons. The rapid spread of the Antonine Plague through Roman legions returning from the front, or the social scapegoating and superstitions that followed the Black Death, illustrate how misinformation and fear can exacerbate the crisis. On the other hand, the successful containment of SARS in 2003 through coordinated global efforts and transparent communication showcases the power of international collaboration and science-based policies.

These lessons are not just of historical interest—they are urgently relevant today. The COVID-19 pandemic has brought to light many of the same challenges faced by our ancestors: the need for rapid response, the dangers of misinformation, and the critical importance of global cooperation. It has also highlighted our modern vulnerabilities, from overreliance on global supply chains to disparities in healthcare access.

A Call to Action

As we navigate the ongoing challenges of the COVID-19 pandemic, it is crucial to look back and learn from the past. This book aims to do just that—by examining pandemics throughout history, we can gain a deeper understanding of the patterns and responses that have shaped human society. This understanding is not merely academic; it is essential for preparing for the future. Pandemics will occur again. The question is not if, but when. And when they do, will we be ready?

We have the tools, the knowledge, and the experience to mitigate the impact of future pandemics. But this requires collective action—by governments, by communities, and by individuals. It requires a commitment to science, to solidarity, and to empathy. It requires us to build robust public health systems, to invest in research and innovation, and to prioritize global cooperation over nationalist agendas.

Your Role in Shaping the Future

As readers, you are not just passive observers of this history. You are part of the ongoing story. The choices we make today—about how we respond to pandemics, how we prepare for future outbreaks, and how we support one another in times of crisis—will shape the world for generations to come. This book is a call to action: to learn, to reflect, and to engage in the collective effort to build a more resilient, equitable, and prepared global society.

Let us not be mere witnesses to the devastation that pandemics can bring. Instead, let us be proactive participants in shaping a world that can withstand these challenges. Let us learn from our history, not just to survive but to thrive in the face of future pandemics. The next chapters will take you through the harrowing tales of pandemics past, the lessons learned, and the steps we must take today to safeguard our future.

Are you ready to join this journey through time, to learn from the past, and to act for the future? The story of pandemics is the story of us all. Together, let us write the next chapter—one of resilience, preparedness, and hope.

Part 1: The Plague of Athens (430 B.C.)

The year was 430 B.C., and Athens, one of the greatest city-states of the ancient world, stood at the zenith of its power. Its walls were formidable, its fleet unmatched, and its culture flourished under the guidance of Pericles, a leader celebrated for his wisdom and vision. Yet, despite its strength and prosperity, Athens was unprepared for the enemy that would soon strike—not an enemy wielding swords or shields, but one invisible and deadly, capable of bringing the mighty city to its knees.

As the summer sun beat down on Athens, an ominous shadow began to spread through its narrow streets and bustling marketplaces. It started with a few isolated cases—men and women who developed strange symptoms, their eyes burning with fever, their throats parched and raw. At first, the city's healers were puzzled but not alarmed. Illness was not uncommon in the crowded quarters of Athens. But soon, it became clear that this was no ordinary sickness.

The Panic Begins

The first signs of widespread panic came when entire households fell ill within days. Families barricaded themselves in their homes, fear etched on their faces as they heard the cries of their neighbors. The symptoms were terrifying: high fever, intense thirst, and unquenchable burning in the stomach. As the disease progressed, victims would vomit bile, their skin breaking out in pustules and ulcers. And then, almost mercifully, came death. Swift, brutal, and seemingly without pattern. It struck young and old, rich and poor, indiscriminately.

Rumors spread faster than the plague itself. Some claimed it was a curse from the gods, a divine punishment for hubris or impiety. Others whispered that it was the work of Athens' enemies, who had somehow poisoned the city's water supply. The uncertainty fueled the panic. The Agora, usually filled with the vibrant hum of traders and philosophers, became a place of whispers and fear. People avoided eye contact, afraid that a single glance could bring the disease upon them.

The Spread and Social Collapse

As the days turned into weeks, the plague spread relentlessly. Athens, now teeming with refugees who had fled the countryside seeking safety behind its walls from the Peloponnesian War, became a cauldron of disease. Overcrowding, poor sanitation, and the sweltering heat created a perfect breeding ground for the sickness. Bodies began to pile up faster than they could be buried. Soon, the city's public burial grounds overflowed, and the dead were left to rot in the streets.

Order collapsed. The intricate social structure that had held Athens together began to disintegrate under the weight of fear and death. Law and piety, once the cornerstones of Athenian society, were discarded in the face of overwhelming despair. People stopped caring for the sick or conducting proper burial rites, violating sacred customs out of sheer terror or resignation. The city, which had once prided itself on its democratic ideals and civic responsibility, now seemed on the brink of anarchy.

The ancient historian Thucydides, himself a survivor of the plague, described the scene in his "History of the Peloponnesian War." His account is chilling: "Men who were half dead already wandered about in delirium; the streets were full of corpses, and death was so common that the dead were left where they fell." Thucydides spoke of how the disease not only ravaged the body but also the spirit of the Athenians. With no hope of survival and no fear of retribution in the afterlife, many turned to hedonism and crime, abandoning all societal norms and moral constraints.

The Unknown Terror

What made the plague particularly terrifying was its mystery. The Athenians had no knowledge of bacteria or viruses; they could not see or understand the enemy that had infiltrated their city. The disease seemed to strike at random, killing some while sparing others, leaving the survivors to grapple with guilt and confusion. Why were some untouched? Was it divine favor, fate, or something else entirely?

Physicians, the healers who were supposed to bring comfort and cure, were among the first to die, struck down in droves as they tried to tend to the sick. Their deaths further eroded public confidence and deepened the sense of helplessness. The more they tried to heal, the faster the disease seemed to spread, as if mocking their efforts. Traditional remedies—herbs, poultices, and prayers—proved useless against the onslaught of the plague. In desperation, some turned to superstition, wearing amulets and charms, or sacrificing animals to the gods. But the plague did not discriminate; it took the devout and the skeptical alike.

As the plague continued to ravage the city, Pericles, the great statesman of Athens, tried to maintain order and morale. He urged the people to stay strong, to not lose faith in their city or themselves. But even he could not escape the scourge. The sight of their leader, once a pillar of strength, weakened and bedridden, further demoralized the population. When Pericles finally succumbed, it seemed to many Athenians that the city's fate was sealed.

Desperate Measures

With no end in sight, the Athenians resorted to desperate measures. Some fled the city, risking death in the hands of Spartan soldiers outside the walls rather than face the plague within. Others sought solace in the temples, praying for deliverance, though even the sanctuaries were not safe from the disease. The priests, too, were dying, and the gods remained silent. The city, once vibrant with life and hope, became a place of shadows and death.

In their desperation, the Athenians tried to find a scapegoat. Foreigners, especially those from regions unaffected by the plague, were blamed and sometimes lynched by angry mobs. Yet these acts of violence brought no relief. The disease continued to spread, unchecked and unstoppable. The very fabric of Athenian society—its values, its beliefs, its social order—was unraveling in the face of this invisible enemy.

A Glimmer of Resilience

Yet, even in the darkest times, there were glimmers of resilience and humanity. Amidst the chaos, some Athenians risked their lives to help others, caring for the sick and burying the dead, often at great personal risk. Thucydides himself noted that those who had recovered from the disease showed great compassion for the afflicted, understanding firsthand the horrors of the plague. These acts of courage and solidarity provided a faint, yet vital, light in an otherwise bleak landscape.

As the summer waned and autumn approached, the plague's grip on Athens slowly began to loosen. Whether due to changes in weather, the natural course of the disease, or simply the exhaustion of its victims, the number of new cases began to decline. The Athenians, battered but not broken, began to emerge from their homes, mourning their dead and contemplating their future. The city was scarred—physically, emotionally, and spiritually—but it had survived.

The Aftermath and Reflection

The plague of Athens would leave deep and lasting scars on the city and its people. It weakened Athens at a critical moment in its conflict with Sparta, contributing to its eventual defeat in the Peloponnesian War. It also led to a profound questioning of the city's values, its leadership, and its gods. The Athenians had always prided themselves on their rationality, their democracy, and their cultural achievements. Yet in the face of the plague, all these seemed fragile and insufficient.

But there was also a lesson in the resilience of the human spirit. Even as the plague tore through Athens, killing tens of thousands and leaving many more bereft, it could not entirely destroy the will of the people. Those who survived carried with them not just the trauma of loss but also the knowledge that they had faced one of the most terrifying events imaginable and had endured. The Athenians would rebuild their city, honor their dead, and continue to strive for greatness, even in the shadow of the plague.

A Legacy of Resilience

The Plague of Athens remains a powerful testament to the resilience of human society in the face of unimaginable adversity. It serves as a stark reminder of how quickly order can dissolve into chaos, how easily fear can turn neighbor against neighbor, and how the invisible forces of nature can humble even the mightiest of civilizations. Yet it also reminds us that even in our darkest moments, there is hope. In the courage of those who cared for the sick, in the determination of a city to rebuild, and in the enduring spirit of humanity to face the unknown with resolve.

As we reflect on the lessons of Athens, we are reminded that history is not just a record of what has happened but a guide to what could be. The story of the Plague of Athens is not just a tale of death and despair—it is a story of survival, of the human capacity to endure, adapt, and, ultimately, prevail. And as we face our own challenges in the modern world, it is a story that resonates now more than ever.

Part 2: The Antonine Plague (165-180 A.D.)

The Roman Empire, at the height of its power in the 2nd century A.D., was an unparalleled force of civilization, culture, and military might. Its borders stretched from the windswept highlands of Britain to the sun-baked deserts of Egypt, encompassing a vast mosaic of peoples, languages, and traditions. The empire's legions were legendary, feared and respected across the known world for their discipline, strategy, and unyielding strength. Yet, in the year 165 A.D., an enemy appeared that even the mightiest Roman legions could not withstand—an enemy invisible to the naked eye, silent, and merciless. This was the Antonine Plague, a mysterious disease that would come to ravage the empire for nearly two decades, leaving in its wake a trail of death, despair, and profound change.

The Mysterious Origins

The origins of the Antonine Plague are shrouded in mystery, much like the disease itself. Historians believe it first emerged in the eastern provinces of the empire, possibly during the Roman campaigns against the Parthians. The legions, having returned from their victories in Mesopotamia, carried with them more than just the spoils of war. As they marched triumphantly back into the heart of Rome, they unknowingly brought a silent killer—a plague that would soon spread across the empire with alarming speed.

At first, the signs were subtle. A few soldiers fell ill, complaining of fever and fatigue. Some dismissed it as the natural toll of war, the body's response to long marches and hard battles. But soon, more began to succumb. The symptoms were unlike anything the Romans had seen before: high fever, diarrhea, vomiting, and a telltale skin eruption that appeared like a rash, spreading rapidly over the body and forming pustules. Within days, the affected would be dead, their bodies covered in dark, purulent sores.

The Spread of Fear and Disease

As the disease spread among the troops, panic began to set in. The legions, the backbone of Roman power and security, were now the unwitting carriers of death. Camps that had once bustled with the disciplined activity of soldiers preparing for battle were now silent, filled with the moans of the sick and dying. The disease did not discriminate between rank or status; commanders and common soldiers alike fell victim. Orders were given to isolate the sick, but the effort proved futile. The disease moved too quickly, and soon, entire units were decimated.

As the legions returned to their home cities, the plague followed. It spread along Rome's vast network of roads and trade routes, moving from town to town, city to city, leaving a trail of death in its wake. The bustling markets of Rome, Antioch, and Alexandria, once filled with merchants from across the empire, became hotbeds of contagion. People began to avoid public places, and the great forums and amphitheaters stood eerily empty, their silence broken only by the cries of the afflicted.

The psychological impact on the Roman population was immense. In a society accustomed to the certainties of law, order, and military might, the sudden appearance of an invisible, unstoppable enemy shattered the Roman psyche. Fear spread faster than the plague itself. Rumors and misinformation abounded. Some believed the disease was a curse from the gods, a punishment for the empire's excesses and impiety. Others whispered that it was a foreign weapon, a deliberate act of biological warfare by Rome's enemies. The once mighty and confident Rome was now a city of fear and uncertainty.

Personal Stories from a Plague-Ravaged Empire

In the midst of this chaos, personal stories emerged that spoke to the human cost of the plague. One such story is that of Lucius, a centurion who had served with distinction in the Parthian campaign. Upon returning to Rome, he was one of the first in his cohort to fall ill. His wife, Julia, a strong-willed woman who had weathered many storms during Lucius's years away at war, found herself alone, caring for her fevered husband. She watched in horror as his condition deteriorated—his skin became mottled with angry red rashes, his breath labored, his body wracked with convulsions.

Desperate, Julia sought help from a local physician, but the man, overwhelmed with patients and lacking any real knowledge of the disease, could offer little more than herbal concoctions and prayers. Lucius's death was quick and brutal. Within days, he was gone, leaving Julia not just a widow, but a woman alone in a city where death lurked at every corner. She watched helplessly as the plague claimed neighbor after neighbor, leaving entire streets deserted.

Julia's story was not unique. Across the empire, families were torn apart by the plague. Children were orphaned, parents buried their offspring, and entire lineages were wiped out. Funerals became a grim commonality, and soon there were too many dead to bury properly. The Romans, who had once prided themselves on their elaborate funeral rites and traditions, were forced to abandon them. Bodies were left in the streets, and mass graves became a necessity. The stench of death hung over Rome, a constant reminder of the empire's vulnerability.

Impact on the Military and the Empire's Stability

The military, long considered the heart of Roman strength, was particularly hard hit. Legions that had once been thousands strong were reduced to mere hundreds. The disease sapped the empire of its soldiers, weakening its defenses at a critical time. Rome's enemies, ever watchful for a sign of weakness, began to stir. Germanic tribes along the Rhine and Danube rivers, sensing opportunity, launched raids across the border. In the east, Parthian forces began to regroup, emboldened by the news of Rome's suffering.

Emperor Marcus Aurelius, a philosopher-king who had long believed in the power of reason and the rule of law, found himself facing an unprecedented crisis. The plague was not just a public health disaster; it was a threat to the very fabric of the empire. Marcus Aurelius sought the counsel of his advisors, but their recommendations varied wildly. Some called for strict quarantines and the closing of the borders, while others argued for a more measured response, fearing the economic consequences of such actions.

The emperor's personal writings, later known as the "Meditations," reveal a man grappling with both the philosophical and practical implications of the plague. He wrote of the fleeting nature of life, the importance of resilience, and the need for wisdom in the face of adversity. Yet, even the stoic philosopher could not ignore the human suffering around him. In a rare display of emotion, he ordered the construction of new hospitals and called for increased support for the families of the dead. But these measures, though compassionate, were insufficient against the scale of the crisis.

The Invisible Enemy

The true horror of the Antonine Plague lay in its invisibility. Unlike Rome's enemies on the battlefield, this foe could not be seen, heard, or easily understood. It did not respect borders, walls, or military might. It slipped past the strongest defenses, infiltrating the most secure cities, striking down generals and slaves alike. The Romans, known for their engineering prowess and military strategy, found themselves at a loss. They had no weapons against this new enemy, no strategies to contain it. The unseen nature of the disease added an element of suspense and terror to the unfolding crisis.

In the face of this invisible enemy, some Romans turned to the gods, seeking divine intervention through rituals, sacrifices, and prayers. Temples were filled with desperate supplicants, hoping to appease the gods and end the suffering. Yet, the gods remained silent. The plague continued unabated, leading to a crisis of faith for many. If the gods could not or would not intervene, then what hope did mortal men have? The philosophical and religious underpinnings of Roman society began to crack under the weight of the plague's devastation.

The Grim Reality of Life in a Plague-Ravaged Rome

Life in plague-ravaged Rome became a grim reality that tested the limits of human endurance and morality. The city's infrastructure, once a marvel of the ancient world, began to collapse under the strain. Food shortages became common as farmers, too, fell victim to the disease. The great aqueducts, which had supplied fresh water to the city's millions, were poorly maintained as workers died or fled. Sewers overflowed, mixing with the unburied dead, creating a stench that permeated the air.

Trade, the lifeblood of the Roman economy, ground to a halt. Ships that once carried grain from Egypt and spices from the East lay idle in the harbors, their crews either dead or too fearful to venture into plague-stricken ports. Markets emptied, and coins lost their value as the economy teetered on the brink of collapse. Starvation loomed as a secondary threat, compounding the misery of a city already stretched to its limits.

And yet, amidst the darkness, there were glimpses of light. Stories of extraordinary bravery and sacrifice emerged, stories of those who risked everything to care for the sick, to comfort the dying, and to bury the dead with dignity. In the heart of the city, the Christian community, still a small and often persecuted minority, distinguished itself by its care for the afflicted. Unlike many, they did not flee the city. Instead, they provided what care they could, sharing their meager resources, offering prayers and solace to the dying. Their actions did not go unnoticed, and for some Romans, these small acts of compassion in a city otherwise paralyzed by fear offered a glimmer of hope.

A Lasting Impact

The Antonine Plague would eventually subside, as all plagues do, but its impact on Rome was profound and lasting. The empire would never be the same. The population loss was staggering; estimates suggest that up to five million people—nearly a quarter of the population—may have died. The social, economic, and military consequences were equally severe, weakening the empire and setting the stage for further instability in the centuries to come.

The plague also left a lasting mark on Roman thought and philosophy. It challenged the traditional Roman stoicism and led to a greater introspection about the nature of life, death, and the divine. It exposed the limits of human power and control, reminding even the mighty Romans that there were forces beyond their comprehension or ability to conquer.

Reflections and Lessons Learned

The Antonine Plague serves as a stark reminder of the fragility of even the most powerful civilizations. It teaches us about the limits of human knowledge and the importance of humility in the face of the unknown. It also underscores the critical role of compassion and community in times of crisis. As we reflect on this dark chapter in Roman history, we are reminded that while we may never fully understand or control the forces of nature, we can choose how we respond to them.

The Antonine Plague was a test of Rome's resilience and adaptability, a test that the empire ultimately survived, though at great cost. It is a story not just of loss, but of endurance, a story that continues to resonate as we face our own challenges in a world where the invisible enemy is always at the gates.

Part 3: The Justinian Plague (541-542 A.D.)

The year was 541 A.D., and the Byzantine Empire was a beacon of civilization in a world fraught with turmoil. Under the rule of Emperor Justinian I, the empire was at the height of its power, seeking to restore the glory of Rome and expand its influence across the Mediterranean. Constantinople, the empire's capital, was a marvel of architectural splendor and cultural achievement. Yet, just as the empire seemed poised to reach even greater heights, an invisible threat emerged from the shadows, a threat that would bring the empire to its knees and change the course of history. This was the Justinian Plague, one of the deadliest pandemics ever recorded, a silent, unseen enemy that would engulf the Byzantine world in fear, death, and chaos.

The Mysterious Emergence

The plague's first signs were subtle, almost imperceptible against the backdrop of a bustling empire. It began in the remote corners of the empire, in small villages and towns along the Nile in Egypt, where reports of a strange illness trickled in. At first, these were dismissed as isolated incidents—unremarkable in an age where disease was a constant companion to human life. But as the weeks passed, the number of cases grew, and the illness showed no signs of abating. The plague moved like a shadow along the trade routes, spreading northwards with a terrifying speed.

By the time the plague reached the port cities of the Mediterranean, it was clear this was no ordinary sickness. The symptoms were brutal and swift. Victims developed sudden fevers, followed by swelling of the lymph nodes in the groin, armpits, or neck—buboes that turned dark and painful, the harbingers of death. Those afflicted often died within days, their bodies wracked with pain, their skin covered in blackened patches from internal hemorrhages. The disease spread rapidly, claiming lives indiscriminately, and soon the port cities, once bustling hubs of commerce and culture, were silent and still, filled only with the cries of the dying.

The Plague Reaches Constantinople

In the spring of 542, the plague arrived in Constantinople, the heart of the Byzantine Empire. The city, famed for its magnificent architecture, its towering walls, and its vibrant marketplaces, was ill-prepared for the silent killer that now lurked within its gates. It is said that the disease arrived on grain ships from Egypt, and once inside the city, it spread like wildfire. The tightly packed neighborhoods, the crowded streets, and the city's bustling ports provided the perfect conditions for the plague to thrive.

At first, the plague struck sporadically, with isolated cases appearing in different quarters of the city. But soon, the number of cases began to rise exponentially. Panic set in as people realized the nature of the threat they faced. Neighbors turned on each other, fearful that contact with the sick would bring death to their own doorsteps. The air was thick with the stench of fear, and the city, once vibrant with life, began to shudder under the weight of impending doom.

The bodies began to pile up, faster than they could be buried. Graveyards overflowed, and soon there was no more room for the dead. The authorities, overwhelmed and unprepared, resorted to mass graves. In the harbor, ships filled with dead sailors and merchants drifted aimlessly, too dangerous to approach, their crews lost to the plague. The city's streets, usually filled with the noise of trade and daily life, fell eerily silent, save for the mournful cries of those who had lost loved ones.

Chaos and Fear in the City

As the plague tightened its grip on Constantinople, the city descended into chaos. The social fabric of the city, already frayed by war and economic hardship, began to unravel completely. Law and order broke down as the death toll mounted. Families were torn apart, with children orphaned and parents left without their offspring. The rich and poor alike fell victim to the disease; wealth and status offered no protection against the invisible enemy. The mighty palaces and grand mansions of the city were filled with the sick and dying, and the once-lavish homes became places of despair and death.

Desperation fueled suspicion, and suspicion bred violence. Foreigners and outsiders were blamed for bringing the plague to the city. Some accused them of witchcraft or poisoning the water supply, leading to mobs forming and innocent lives being taken in the frantic search for someone to blame. But there was no escaping the truth—the plague respected no boundaries, knew no limits, and cared nothing for human prejudice.

Religious leaders, too, struggled to provide answers. The people turned to the Church, seeking solace in faith and the hope that God might intervene to save them. Prayers were offered, and processions were held in the streets, but the plague continued unabated. The priests, like the physicians, could do little more than offer comfort to the dying. Some saw the plague as divine retribution, a punishment for the sins of the city, while others believed it was a test of their faith. In either case, the people of Constantinople were caught in a struggle not just for their lives, but for their souls.

Economic Devastation

The impact of the Justinian Plague on the Byzantine economy was catastrophic. The city, the beating heart of a vast trading empire, came to a standstill. The marketplaces, once thronged with merchants from across the Mediterranean, were deserted. The ports, usually filled with ships bearing goods from distant lands, were eerily quiet. Trade ground to a halt as fear of the plague spread faster than the disease itself. The intricate web of commerce that had sustained the empire for centuries began to unravel, and with it, the economic stability of the Byzantine world.

The labor force was decimated. Farmers, unable to tend to their fields, saw their crops wither and die. Artisans, once the lifeblood of the city's economy, were struck down, leaving workshops empty and production halted. The tax base, the foundation of imperial revenue, crumbled as the plague swept through the countryside, claiming the lives of those who worked the land and filled the empire's coffers. The economic consequences were not just immediate but would be felt for generations to come, weakening the empire's ability to defend itself and maintain its vast territories.

Personal Stories of Tragedy and Loss

Amidst the widespread death and despair, personal stories emerged that spoke to the human cost of the plague. One such story is that of Theodora, a young mother who lived in the bustling district of Constantinople's harbor. Her husband, Andreas, was a merchant who traded in spices from the East. When the plague arrived, Andreas was among the first to fall ill. Theodora, unable to find help, cared for him as best she could, watching helplessly as the disease ravaged his body. He died within days, leaving Theodora alone with their two small children.

As the plague spread, Theodora's children, too, fell ill. In desperation, she carried them through the deserted streets to the nearest church, hoping for a miracle. But there were no miracles to be found in plague-ravaged Constantinople. The priests, overwhelmed and fearful for their own lives, could offer little more than a prayer. Within a week, Theodora had lost her entire family. Her story, one of thousands, captures the grim reality faced by so many—lives torn apart, families destroyed, and communities left in tatters.

The Emperor's Response

Emperor Justinian, a ruler who had once dreamed of restoring the Roman Empire to its former glory, found himself grappling with an unprecedented crisis. The plague struck at the very heart of his ambitions, threatening not just his rule, but the stability of the entire empire. Justinian himself fell ill, bedridden with fever and fear, but he miraculously recovered, emerging from his illness with a renewed determination to save his empire.

In a desperate bid to maintain order and restore confidence, Justinian enacted a series of measures aimed at curbing the spread of the disease and managing the crisis. He ordered the construction of mass graves outside the city walls and mandated that all bodies be buried within three days of death, hoping to prevent the further spread of the disease. He also commissioned new hospitals and called for the redistribution of grain to prevent famine.

But even these measures, though well-intentioned, proved largely ineffective against the scale of the disaster. The plague's reach was too vast, its impact too severe. Despite his efforts, Justinian was unable to prevent the collapse of the city's social and economic order. The empire, once a beacon of civilization and power, was now a shadow of its former self, ravaged by an enemy it could neither see nor understand.

The Eerie Silence After the Peak

As the plague reached its peak, the streets of Constantinople were filled with an eerie silence. The once vibrant city, known for its lively markets, grand processions, and endless activity, was now a city of the dead. The sound of laughter and conversation was replaced by the cries of the dying and the silence of the abandoned. The great Hagia Sophia, once filled with worshippers, stood empty and still, its grand dome echoing with the mournful prayers of a few remaining priests.

The silence was perhaps the most terrifying of all. It was the silence of a city that had lost its spirit, a city whose people were too afraid to hope, too broken to rebuild. The air, thick with the stench of death, hung heavy over the city, a constant reminder of the devastation that had been wrought. Those who survived did so with a deep sense of loss and a lingering fear of what might come next.

The Aftermath and Long-Term Consequences

The Justinian Plague eventually began to recede
, its intensity waning as quickly as it had risen. But its impact on the Byzantine Empire was profound and long-lasting. The population loss was staggering; some estimates suggest that up to 25 million people may have died across the empire. The economic repercussions were severe, with entire regions left depopulated and economically devastated. The military, too, was weakened, its ranks thinned by the disease, leaving the empire vulnerable to external threats.

The plague also had a profound impact on the cultural and religious landscape of the empire. The widespread death and suffering led to a crisis of faith for many. The Church, which had been seen as a source of solace and stability, was unable to provide answers or relief. This led to a rise in apocalyptic thinking and a shift towards more austere forms of religious expression. The once cosmopolitan and culturally rich Constantinople became a city marked by suspicion, fear, and a focus on survival.

Reflections on the Justinian Plague

The Justinian Plague stands as a stark reminder of the vulnerability of even the most powerful civilizations to the forces of nature. It is a story of a city, an empire, and a people brought to their knees by a foe they could neither see nor understand. It is a story of fear, chaos, and death, but also one of resilience and survival. For even in the darkest days of the plague, there were those who found the strength to endure, to care for others, and to rebuild.

The plague would leave an indelible mark on the Byzantine Empire, shaping its history and influencing its future. It serves as a reminder that even in the face of unimaginable adversity, there is always hope. And it is this hope, this resilience that ultimately defines the human spirit.

As we look back on the Justinian Plague, we are reminded of the fragility of life and the importance of community, compassion, and resilience in the face of crisis. The lessons of Constantinople in 541 A.D. are not just for the history books—they are lessons for all of us, in every age, as we face our own challenges and strive to build a better, more resilient world.

Part 4: The Black Death (1347-1351)

In the mid-14th century, Europe was a land of bustling cities, flourishing trade, and growing populations. The vibrant exchange of goods and ideas had created a period of economic prosperity and cultural development. However, beneath this veneer of growth and stability, there lurked an unseen threat, one that would arrive suddenly and with devastating force, forever altering the course of European history. This was the Black Death, one of the most catastrophic pandemics ever to strike humankind, a disease that would unleash unprecedented terror and suffering across cities and villages, leaving a continent scarred and a society forever changed.

The Arrival: A Shadow over Europe

The Black Death arrived in Europe in 1347, borne across the Mediterranean by trade ships traveling from the East. It is believed to have originated in the arid plains of Central Asia, where it made its way to Europe along the Silk Road, facilitated by the movement of armies, traders, and caravans. The disease, caused by the bacterium *Yersinia pestis*, was carried by fleas that infested black rats, common stowaways on merchant ships. The first recorded outbreak in Europe occurred in the port city of Messina in Sicily.

In October of 1347, a fleet of Genoese trading ships docked at Messina, their sails torn and their crew gravely ill. The sailors, covered in mysterious black boils oozing blood and pus, were barely alive. The city authorities, horrified by the sight, ordered the ships out of the harbor, but it was already too late. The plague had come ashore. Within days, it spread through the crowded streets of Messina, leaving death and panic in its wake.

News of the terrible disease traveled quickly, but even as word spread of its arrival, few could comprehend the magnitude of the disaster that was about to unfold. From Sicily, the plague spread rapidly, moving northward into mainland Italy. It reached the bustling cities of Genoa, Venice, and Florence, where it quickly took root. The disease moved with terrifying speed along Europe's trade routes, carried by merchants, pilgrims, and soldiers. By the spring of 1348, it had crossed into France and spread into Spain, England, and beyond.

The Spread and Growing Fear

The spread of the Black Death was relentless, like a shadow creeping across the continent. The disease manifested in two primary forms: the bubonic plague, characterized by swollen lymph nodes or buboes, fever, chills, and vomiting; and the pneumonic plague, which infected the lungs, causing violent coughing and, more often than not, a swift death. Both forms were terrifying, and both spread like wildfire through Europe's towns and villages.

As the plague advanced, fear gripped the land. In city after city, the streets filled with the dead and dying. Bodies lay in doorways, markets, and public squares, left unattended as the living were too afraid to approach. The usual sounds of urban life—the chatter of merchants, the clatter of horses, the hum of daily activity—fell silent, replaced by the mournful wails of the grieving and the ceaseless tolling of church bells announcing yet another death. The cities of Europe, once centers of trade and culture, became eerie, silent places, their inhabitants hiding indoors, hoping to escape the invisible killer.

In rural villages, the situation was no better. Farmers and peasants, cut off from the news of the cities, were often taken by surprise when the disease arrived. Entire communities were wiped out within days, their bodies left to rot in the fields and houses. Stories of ghost villages spread—places where every inhabitant had died, leaving behind only the buildings as silent witnesses to the catastrophe. Travel between villages and towns nearly ceased as people became afraid to leave their homes or welcome outsiders, fearing that anyone could bring death to their doorstep.

Suspense and Terror: The Mystery of the Plague

What made the Black Death particularly terrifying was its mystery. Medieval Europeans had no understanding of bacteria, viruses, or the mechanisms of disease transmission. They could not see their enemy, could not predict its movements, and had no way to defend themselves. All they knew was that the plague struck without warning and spared no one. The wealthy died alongside the poor, the pious alongside the sinner. No amount of money, status, or faith seemed to offer protection.

In the absence of understanding, fear bred superstition and rumor. Some believed the plague was a punishment from God, a divine retribution for the sins of humanity. Others blamed outsiders—Jews, Romani, lepers, or foreigners—suspecting them of poisoning wells or casting curses. These beliefs often led to violent persecution and massacres, as terrified communities sought to rid themselves of those they saw as the cause of their suffering.

In Strasbourg, for example, a city in the Holy Roman Empire, the local Jewish community was accused of causing the plague by poisoning the water supply. In February 1349, over 1,000 Jews were burned alive by their neighbors in a horrific act of mass violence driven by fear and ignorance. Similar events occurred across Europe, adding another layer of tragedy to an already dire situation.

The Horror of Mass Graves

As the death toll mounted, traditional burial practices were abandoned. There were simply too many dead and not enough living to bury them. Mass graves were dug outside city walls, filled with bodies piled one on top of the other. In some places, the dead were left in the streets, covered in quicklime to reduce the stench of decay. The sight of mass graves and unburied bodies became commonplace, a grim reminder of the scale of the disaster.

In Florence, one of Italy's wealthiest cities, the chronicler Giovanni Boccaccio described the horror in vivid detail: "The plight of the lower and most of the middle class was pitiable to behold. They fell sick by the thousands, and seeing they had no help from physicians, they died, often without a witness. Many died in the open streets, others dying in their houses made it known by the stench of their rotting bodies." His account, like many others from the period, paints a picture of a city overwhelmed by death and decay, where fear and despair reigned.

Personal Stories of Suffering and Survival

Amid the widespread suffering, individual stories of tragedy and resilience emerged, capturing the human dimension of the Black Death. In the English village of Walsham, the plague arrived in the late summer of 1349. Agnes, a young mother of three, watched helplessly as her husband, John, fell ill. Within days, he developed the telltale symptoms: fever, vomiting, and the dreaded buboes. Despite her best efforts, Agnes could do nothing to save him. John died within a week, leaving Agnes alone to care for their children.

But the plague was not finished with Agnes's family. Soon after her husband's death, her eldest son, William, also fell ill. Agnes, already grieving and exhausted, nursed him as best she could, but the disease took him too. Her remaining children, Thomas and Joan, were terrified, clinging to their mother as the plague swept through their village, claiming the lives of their neighbors and friends.

In her despair, Agnes considered fleeing the village, but there was nowhere to go. She had heard that the plague was everywhere, in every town and city. So, she stayed, tending to her children and praying for their safety. Against all odds, Thomas and Joan survived. When the plague finally passed, leaving Walsham a shadow of its former self, Agnes and her two surviving children were among the few left standing. Her story, like many others, is one of both tragedy and resilience—a testament to the strength of the human spirit in the face of unimaginable adversity.

Understanding and Coping with the Unknown

As the plague continued to ravage Europe, people sought to understand and cope with the disaster in whatever ways they could. Physicians, though powerless against the disease, offered their theories and remedies, ranging from bloodletting to potions made from exotic herbs. None were effective, but in a time of desperate need, people were willing to try anything.

Religious fervor increased as well. Some saw the plague as a sign of the end times, while others believed it was a test of faith. Flagellant movements, where groups of people would publicly whip themselves as a form of penance, spread across Europe. These groups believed that by mortifying their flesh, they could atone for the sins of the world and bring an end to the plague. Yet, despite their fervor, the plague continued, undeterred by human suffering or sacrifice.

In some places, however, the fear gave way to resilience. In Milan, Italy, the city authorities took a different approach to the plague. When the first cases appeared, they immediately quarantined the infected and their families, sealing them in their homes to prevent the disease's spread. Harsh and draconian as this measure was, it proved effective. While other cities saw their populations decimated, Milan's losses were significantly lower. This action, while controversial, showed that understanding and discipline could mitigate the impact of the disease, even if it could not stop it entirely.

The Eerie Silence and Aftermath

By the time the Black Death had run its course around 1351, it had claimed the lives of an estimated 25 to 30 million people in Europe—about one-third of the continent's population. Entire regions were depopulated, cities were left in ruins, and the social and economic structures that had supported medieval life were irrevocably altered.

The silence that followed the plague was haunting. Fields lay fallow, villages were abandoned, and the once-crowded cities were eerily empty. The survivors, those who had lived through the nightmare, were left to pick up the pieces of a shattered world.

The labor shortage caused by the massive loss of life led to economic and social changes, including the end of serfdom in some regions as labor became more valuable and workers demanded better conditions and wages.

The Church, which had been unable to provide answers or protection, faced a crisis of confidence. Many people, disillusioned by the inability of their religious leaders to explain or stop the plague, began to question long-held beliefs. This erosion of faith in traditional institutions would sow the seeds of change, eventually contributing to the social and religious upheavals that marked the later centuries.

Yet, there was also resilience. New art forms emerged that reflected the trauma of the plague years, from the macabre imagery of the "Danse Macabre" to the introspective and somber tones of post-plague literature and music. The

Black Death, in its wake, left not just death and despair, but also a new Europe, one marked by both loss and a newfound resilience.

A Legacy of Fear and Strength

The Black Death remains one of the most defining events in European history. It was a catastrophe that brought unimaginable suffering, but it was also a crucible of resilience and change. In the face of an unseen, unstoppable enemy, people sought to understand, to survive, and ultimately to rebuild. The terror and the silence of the plague years are a testament to the fragility of human life and the strength of the human spirit.

As we reflect on the Black Death, we are reminded of the lessons of fear and hope, despair and resilience. The plague may have passed, but its impact on European society, culture, and history endures, a haunting reminder of the power of nature and the enduring strength of humanity in the face of adversity.

Part 5: The Columbian Exchange and Native American Pandemics (15th-16th Century)

The Columbian Exchange, a term used to describe the profound exchange of goods, ideas, plants, animals, and diseases between the Old World and the New following Christopher Columbus's voyages, was one of the most significant events in world history. It marked the beginning of a new era of global interaction, but it also set in motion a series of tragic events that would forever change the Americas. While the exchange brought new crops, livestock, and technologies to the New World, it also introduced a devastating array of diseases to Native American populations—smallpox, measles, influenza, and others—that would decimate entire societies and lead to dramatic cultural and demographic shifts.

The Silent Invaders

Before 1492, the Americas were home to a diverse array of indigenous civilizations, from the advanced agricultural societies of Mesoamerica and the Andes to the hunter-gatherer communities of North America. These societies had developed rich cultures, complex social structures, and sophisticated knowledge systems, yet they had been largely isolated from the rest of the world for thousands of years. As a result, they had no immunity to the diseases that were common in Europe, Asia, and Africa.

When European explorers and colonists arrived, they unknowingly brought with them an invisible and deadly arsenal of pathogens. Diseases such as smallpox, measles, typhus, and influenza had long been endemic in the Old World, where repeated outbreaks had shaped human immunity over centuries. But in the New World, these pathogens found a virgin population with no previous exposure and no defense.

The first recorded outbreak of Old World diseases in the Americas occurred shortly after Columbus's arrival in 1492. Within decades, the effects were catastrophic. Entire communities were laid waste, their populations reduced by as much as 90% in some regions. The spread of these diseases was swift and brutal, moving along trade routes and rivers, across mountains and plains, often arriving in new areas ahead of European explorers. The indigenous peoples, seeing their families and neighbors fall ill with no explanation and no cure, were plunged into confusion and despair.

The Suspense and Confusion of First Encounters

Imagine the first encounters between Native American communities and these new, invisible invaders. In villages and cities across the Americas, people began to fall ill with strange symptoms. In the Aztec capital of Tenochtitlán, the great city on the lake, rumors spread of a mysterious illness sweeping through the population. Men and women who had been healthy only days before were suddenly stricken with high fevers, painful rashes, and a relentless cough. Bodies swelled with pustules that burst and oozed, leaving the skin raw and bleeding. The death was swift, and the disease spread faster than wildfire.

The Aztecs, like many Native American communities, had no understanding of the germs that were causing these illnesses. They could not see the enemy they were fighting; they could only see the devastating effects. Healers, who had traditionally used herbs and spiritual rituals to cure ailments, found their skills useless against this new sickness. In their desperation, many communities turned to their gods, performing ceremonies and sacrifices in hopes of appeasing angry deities. Yet, the diseases continued unabated, striking down young and old, strong and weak alike.

The confusion was not just physical but psychological. These diseases undermined the very fabric of Native American societies, challenging their understanding of the world and their place within it. Traditional knowledge systems and belief structures, which had served these communities for generations, were suddenly insufficient in the face of an unseen, unexplainable threat. This confusion and fear were exacerbated by the simultaneous arrival of European colonists, whose presence was often interpreted as either a curse or a test sent by the gods.

Tragic Realities: The Decimation of Populations

The impact of these diseases on Native American populations was nothing short of apocalyptic. In some regions, entire communities were wiped out within a matter of years. In the Caribbean, where Columbus first landed, the indigenous Taíno population was decimated. Once numbering in the hundreds of thousands, the Taíno were reduced to a few hundred survivors within a generation, their society and culture all but erased.

On the mainland, the story was similar. The once-thriving cities of the Maya, Aztec, and Inca empires were ravaged by successive waves of epidemics. In the Andes, the Inca Empire was struck by a devastating smallpox outbreak shortly before the arrival of Francisco Pizarro. The disease killed the emperor, Huayna Capac, leading to a succession crisis that weakened the empire and made it vulnerable to Spanish conquest. In Mesoamerica, smallpox spread rapidly through the Aztec Empire following the arrival of Hernán Cortés. The Aztecs, already weakened by internal strife and warfare with the Spanish, were brought to their knees by the disease, which killed tens of thousands and left the survivors demoralized and disoriented.

The North American continent, too, was not spared. The diseases moved swiftly among the tribes of the Eastern Woodlands and Great Plains. From the powerful Iroquois Confederacy in the Northeast to the Mandan villages along the Missouri River, the toll was immense. It is estimated that between 1492 and 1600, as much as 90% of the indigenous population of the Americas may have died as a result of these diseases—a demographic collapse unparalleled in human history.

Cultural and Demographic Shifts

The massive loss of life led to dramatic cultural and demographic shifts across the Americas. Entire societies were disrupted or destroyed. In many places, traditional social structures collapsed as leaders and elders, who were often among the first to die, left behind communities without guidance or governance. The loss of so many people in such a short time created a vacuum that would reshape the cultural landscape of the Americas.

In some regions, the devastation was so complete that survivors were forced to abandon their homes, their fields, and their traditions, moving in search of refuge and new beginnings. This led to a period of profound migration and movement, as communities fragmented and reformed in response to the new realities. For some, this meant integrating with neighboring groups, forming new alliances, and adopting new cultural practices. For others, it meant isolation and retreat, as they sought to protect what remained of their communities from further exposure.

The introduction of European livestock, crops, and technologies also had a transformative effect on Native American societies. Horses, brought by the Spanish, would eventually revolutionize the way of life for many Plains tribes, who adapted their cultures to a new, nomadic existence centered around hunting bison. New crops, such as wheat and barley, altered agricultural practices and diets. These changes, while significant, were often overshadowed by the sheer scale of loss and trauma caused by the diseases.

Personal Stories of Suffering and Survival

Among the countless stories of suffering and survival during this period, one stands out—that of a young Nahua woman named Tecuichpotzin, the daughter of the Aztec Emperor Moctezuma II. When the Spanish arrived in Tenochtitlán, Tecuichpotzin was a princess, living a life of privilege within the palace walls. But her world was soon turned upside down as the Spanish conquest began.

Her father was taken captive by Hernán Cortés, and the city erupted in chaos. As the siege of Tenochtitlán dragged on, smallpox swept through the city, killing tens of thousands, including her father. Tecuichpotzin, now orphaned, witnessed the collapse of her civilization. She survived the epidemic and, after the Spanish victory, was baptized and married off to a Spanish conquistador. She would go on to marry several more times, each marriage a political alliance aimed at solidifying Spanish rule. Tecuichpotzin's life, marked by loss, adaptation, and survival, embodies the profound transformations faced by Native American societies during this tumultuous period.

In North America, another story of survival emerged from the Mandan village along the Missouri River. The Mandan, known for their earth lodges and vibrant trade networks, were hit hard by smallpox in the late 18th century, a wave that echoed the earlier tragedies of the 16th century. A Mandan woman named Buffalo Bird Woman, who survived one of the later outbreaks, recounted the devastating effects of the disease on her community. Her stories, passed down through oral tradition and later recorded by ethnographers, tell of a world transformed by disease, a society struggling to preserve its traditions and identity in the face of overwhelming loss.

The Psychological Impact: Coping with Catastrophe

The psychological impact of these pandemics on Native American communities was immense. The sudden and inexplicable loss of so many lives created a deep sense of trauma and grief. Traditional practices, beliefs, and cosmologies were challenged in unprecedented ways. For many, the arrival of Europeans and their diseases was seen as a cosmic event, a turning point in their history that required new interpretations and responses.

Some communities interpreted the pandemics as a sign of divine displeasure or as a test of their cultural and spiritual resilience. Rituals, dances, and ceremonies were adapted to address the new realities, and new religious movements emerged. In the American Southwest, for instance, the introduction of European diseases contributed to the development of new Pueblo spiritual practices that sought to understand and mitigate the effects of these catastrophic changes.

Resilience and Adaptation

Despite the overwhelming loss and trauma, Native American societies showed remarkable resilience and adaptability. They adapted to new circumstances, forged new alliances, and redefined their cultural identities in response to the changing world. In many regions, communities rebuilt and recovered, incorporating new elements into their cultures while retaining a strong sense of their heritage and identity.

In the face of the catastrophic impact of European diseases, Native American societies demonstrated a remarkable capacity for adaptation. They engaged in cultural synthesis, blending traditional practices with new elements introduced by Europeans. This process of adaptation was not without its challenges or losses, but it also speaks to the enduring strength and resilience of these communities.

A Legacy of Tragedy and Survival

The introduction of European diseases to the Americas is one of the most tragic aspects of the Columbian Exchange. It resulted in the deaths of millions and the destruction of countless cultures. Yet, it also led to a period of profound transformation and adaptation. Native American societies, despite the immense challenges they faced, did not simply disappear; they adapted, survived, and continued to evolve.

The legacy of this period is a complex one, marked by both profound loss and incredible resilience. It serves as a powerful reminder of the interconnectedness of human societies and the far-reaching consequences of contact and exchange. The story of the Columbian Exchange and the pandemics that followed is not just a story of disease and death, but also of survival, adaptation, and the enduring strength of the human spirit.

Part 6: The Great Plague of London (1665-1666)

In the sweltering summer of 1665, the city of London was a bustling metropolis, its streets teeming with merchants, craftsmen, and ordinary citizens going about their daily lives. The city was growing rapidly, its population swelled by an influx of people seeking work and opportunity. But beneath this veneer of prosperity lay the dark, narrow alleyways and crowded tenements of the poorer districts—breeding grounds for disease. As the hot months stretched on, an unseen enemy began to stalk the city, one that would bring death to thousands and leave an indelible mark on the capital. This was the Great Plague of London, a disease that would grip the city in a vice of fear, suspicion, and death.

The First Signs: A Silent Stalker

The first whispers of the plague came in the spring of 1665. In the crowded parish of St. Giles-in-the-Fields, a few cases of a strange, lethal sickness began to surface. The disease presented itself with sudden chills, followed by fever and a terrifying eruption of painful, blackened buboes in the groin, armpits, and neck. Those afflicted often died within days, their bodies contorted in agony. At first, the cases were few, isolated to the poorest parts of the city. But as spring turned to summer, the numbers began to rise. The plague, it seemed, had come again to London.

Panic spread quickly through the narrow streets. The memories of past outbreaks lingered in the collective consciousness, a grim reminder of the horrors that such an outbreak could bring. As the death toll rose, so did the fear. Neighbors avoided each other, shops began to close, and the wealthy started to flee the city, seeking refuge in the countryside, far from the miasma of death that seemed to hang over London.

The air was thick with rumors. Some said the disease was a punishment from God, a divine retribution for the sins of the city's inhabitants. Others whispered that it had been brought by foreign traders or that it was the work of sorcery. Whatever the cause, one thing was certain: London was in the grip of a deadly plague, and no one was safe.

The Spread Through Crowded Streets

As the summer heat intensified, the plague spread with terrifying speed through London's densely packed neighborhoods. The city's layout, with its narrow, winding streets and overpopulated districts, provided the perfect conditions for the disease to flourish. Fleas, which carried the bacterium *Yersinia pestis* from rat to human, thrived in the unsanitary conditions of the city's poorest quarters. In the narrow alleyways of places like Whitechapel and Cripplegate, the plague found easy prey.

Every day, the cries of the sick and dying echoed through the streets, mingling with the tolling of church bells, which rang incessantly to mark the passing of souls. The death carts began to make their rounds, their drivers calling out in mournful tones, "Bring out your dead!" Families, too afraid to touch their deceased loved ones, would leave them at their doorsteps, hastily retreating back inside to avoid contact with the corpse. The dead, often wrapped in simple shrouds, were piled onto the carts and taken away to mass graves, where they were buried in pits, layer upon layer, and the earth struggling to swallow the city's mounting losses.

Amidst this chaos, the wealthy and powerful sought to protect themselves. King Charles II and his court fled the city for Hampton Court and then further to Oxford, leaving the city in the hands of local officials. The exodus of the elite left a leadership vacuum, with those remaining struggling to maintain order amidst the growing fear and desperation.

The Atmosphere of Fear and Suspicion

The atmosphere in London grew increasingly tense and paranoid. As the plague spread, suspicion fell on those perceived as outsiders or those who might carry the disease. Foreigners, beggars, and even physicians were eyed with distrust. Every stranger was a potential carrier, every cough or sneeze a harbinger of death. The city's residents, already on edge, began to turn on one another, their fear feeding a growing hysteria.

In the neighborhoods hardest hit by the plague, the streets were deserted save for the occasional sight of a solitary figure moving hurriedly, their face covered with a cloth. People avoided each other's gaze, crossing the street to avoid passing too close. Doors were marked with a painted red cross, a signal that someone inside was infected. These houses, sealed shut by the orders of the city's aldermen, became tombs for the living and the dead alike.

Inside one such house lived Thomas, a cobbler in the district of Bishopsgate. When his wife, Margaret, fell ill, he knew there was little hope. He tried to care for her, bringing her water and cool cloths to soothe her fevered brow, but nothing could alleviate her suffering. As her condition worsened, Thomas's fear turned to despair. The aldermen arrived, marking his door with the Red Cross and nailing it shut. Trapped inside with his dying wife and their young daughter, Thomas could only wait, helpless, as the plague claimed his family one by one.

Desperate Measures and Government Struggles

As the plague continued its relentless march through the city, the government struggled to maintain control and prevent complete social collapse. The Lord Mayor and the aldermen implemented a series of draconian measures aimed at curbing the spread of the disease. Houses where the plague was present were to be shut up, with all inhabitants sealed inside for a period of 40 days. Watchmen were stationed outside to ensure no one entered or left. This measure, while intended to contain the disease, often condemned entire households to death.

Orders were given for the slaughter of stray dogs and cats, which were believed to spread the disease. Public gatherings were banned, and markets were shut down. Theaters, usually filled with lively performances, were closed, their stages now empty and dark. The once vibrant city was transformed into a place of silence and fear, its streets echoing with the sounds of death.

But these measures, however well-intentioned, often did little to stem the tide of the plague. The disease spread too quickly, too silently. The city's coffers, strained by the economic impact of the plague, began to run dry. Resources were stretched thin, and the public's patience wore even thinner. As the death toll climbed, the city's leadership faced increasing criticism and unrest. There were riots and protests, with mobs forming outside the homes of those thought to be harboring the sick or hoarding food. The fragile social order of the city was beginning to fray.

Personal Accounts: Life and Death in Plague-Ridden London

Among the many stories of suffering and resilience was that of Mary Vincent, a seamstress in the parish of St. Olave's. Mary, who had lost her husband to the plague in June, found herself alone, caring for her three children. As the weeks passed and the plague drew closer to her street, she watched with growing dread as her neighbors fell ill, their homes marked with the dreaded Red Cross. Her own house, though untouched by the disease, became a place of confinement, as she kept her children inside, away from the deadly air that seemed to swirl outside.

Mary's daily life was filled with anxiety and routine. She boiled vinegar to disinfect the house, burned aromatic herbs to purify the air, and prayed fervently for deliverance. Her children, sensing her fear, remained quiet and subdued, their usual playfulness replaced by a solemn understanding of the danger that surrounded them. One morning, as Mary stood by the window, she saw the death cart trundling down the street, its driver calling out in his mournful voice. She shuddered, pulling her children close, hoping and praying that they would be spared.

Not everyone was as fortunate as Mary and her family. In another part of the city, a young apprentice named Samuel lost his entire family to the plague. His master, a merchant, had succumbed to the disease early on, followed by his wife and two young sons. Samuel, left alone in the empty house, wandered the deserted streets, lost and aimless. He eventually found work helping with the death carts, a grim task but one that provided him with some sense of purpose amidst the chaos. Every day, he loaded the bodies onto the cart, their faces covered with linen shrouds, their limbs stiff and cold. He became numb to the sight and smell of death, his only thought being survival in a city that seemed to have abandoned all hope.

The Haunting Aftermath

By the autumn of 1666, the worst of the plague had passed, leaving behind a city scarred and traumatized. The death toll was staggering; estimates suggest that as many as 100,000 Londoners—nearly a quarter of the city's population—perished in the Great Plague. The streets, once filled with life and activity, were now eerily quiet. Many homes stood empty, their occupants gone, their windows boarded up.

The economic impact was severe. Trade had come to a near standstill, and the city's economy was in ruins. The once-thriving markets and shops remained shuttered, their owners either dead or ruined. The social fabric of London had been stretched to its breaking point, and the city's leaders were faced with the monumental task of rebuilding not just the city's infrastructure, but also its spirit.

The Great Fire of London in September 1666, coming so soon after the plague, was seen by some as both a further curse and a divine cleansing. The fire destroyed much of the city's medieval core, including many of the cramped, plague-ridden alleys and tenements. While the fire brought further destruction, it also marked the beginning of a new chapter in London's history—a chance to rebuild a city scarred by plague and fire into something new.

Reflections on Resilience and Renewal

The Great Plague of London was a tragedy that tested the resilience of its people and the limits of its social and political structures. It revealed both the vulnerability and the strength of the human spirit in the face of overwhelming adversity. While the plague brought immense suffering, it also led to significant changes in public health practices and urban planning. The experience of the plague highlighted the importance of sanitation, quarantine, and disease prevention—lessons that would be remembered in the centuries to come.

As we look back on the Great Plague, we are reminded of the fragility of life and the strength of community. The stories of Mary, Samuel, and countless others who lived through this dark chapter in London's history are a testament to the power of resilience, hope, and the enduring human spirit.

Part 7: The Third Cholera Pandemic (1852-1860)

The Third Cholera Pandemic, which raged between 1852 and 1860, was one of the deadliest outbreaks of cholera in history. Originating in the dense, bustling cities of India, the disease spread rapidly across continents, reaching the farthest corners of the world. Cholera, a disease that could kill within hours of the first symptoms, caused widespread panic, confusion, and death, laying bare the vulnerabilities of burgeoning industrial cities and challenging contemporary understanding of disease transmission. It was during this pandemic that a pivotal discovery would change the course of public health forever.

Origins in India: The Birthplace of a Killer

Cholera, a bacterial infection caused by *Vibrio cholerae*, thrives in conditions of poor sanitation and contaminated water. The disease had been present in the Indian subcontinent for centuries, but the Third Pandemic marked its most widespread and deadly manifestation. The Ganges Delta, with its dense population and inadequate sanitation, was the epicenter. From there, the disease spread rapidly along trade routes and with the movement of troops and pilgrims. British colonial rule facilitated this spread, as the British Empire's extensive networks of commerce and governance unwittingly became conduits for the disease.

The first reports of the outbreak came from Bengal in 1852, where thousands perished in a matter of weeks. The disease moved quickly, flowing like a deadly river through the veins of India's trade routes. As it spread, cholera began to reach other parts of Asia, the Middle East, and eventually Europe, carried by ships and overland caravans. The disease's sudden appearance in distant locations added to the confusion and fear, with many struggling to understand how a sickness could move so swiftly and with such deadly efficiency.

The Grim March across Continents

By 1853, cholera had spread to Persia, where it claimed thousands of lives. From there, it moved into Russia, sweeping through towns and cities, and leaving a trail of death in its wake. Moscow and St. Petersburg, two of Russia's most important cities, saw their populations decimated by the disease. The streets of Moscow, usually filled with the clamor of markets and the bustle of city life, were now filled with the cries of the dying and the silence of fear. In St. Petersburg, the imperial capital, hospitals overflowed with the sick, and the city's sanitation systems, already inadequate, collapsed under the strain.

The disease did not stop there. It continued westward, reaching the Ottoman Empire and North Africa, where it struck Alexandria and Cairo with devastating force. By 1854, cholera had crossed into Europe, wreaking havoc in major cities such as Paris and London. The scenes in European cities were equally grim. Hospitals were overwhelmed with patients, and the streets were lined with bodies waiting to be buried. The stench of death hung over the cities, a grim reminder of the pandemic's deadly grip.

In London, the heart of the British Empire, the arrival of cholera sent shockwaves through the population. The city, already grappling with overcrowding, poor sanitation, and the squalid conditions of its poorest districts, was ripe for an outbreak. The Thames River, a source of drinking water for many of the city's inhabitants, was heavily polluted with raw sewage, a perfect breeding ground for the cholera bacteria. As the disease spread through the city's cramped streets and alleys, fear and confusion took hold.

The Confusion and Fear over Cholera's Cause

At the time, the cause of cholera was poorly understood. The prevailing theory among physicians and scientists was the "miasma" theory—the belief that diseases were spread by "bad air" emanating from rotting organic matter. This theory, widely accepted in medical and scientific circles, posited that the foul smells rising from decaying waste and stagnant water carried disease into the lungs of those who inhaled it. As a result, efforts to combat cholera focused on improving air quality rather than addressing the true source of the infection: contaminated water.

This misunderstanding led to a host of ineffective and sometimes harmful measures. Authorities ordered the burning of tar in the streets and the cleaning of sewers and cesspools to reduce foul odors. People carried handkerchiefs soaked in camphor or other aromatic substances to ward off the "bad air." Yet, despite these efforts, cholera continued to spread, seemingly undeterred by attempts to purify the air. The lack of understanding only added to the fear and confusion, as people saw their neighbors and loved ones struck down by a disease they could neither see nor comprehend.

In the slums of London's East End, where cholera struck hardest, the effects were devastating. Families were torn apart, and entire streets fell silent as the disease moved from house to house. In one tenement, a young mother named Elizabeth watched helplessly as her husband, John, fell ill with the telltale symptoms—violent diarrhea, vomiting, and severe dehydration that left him writhing in agony. She tried to comfort him, but within hours, his condition had deteriorated to the point where he was unrecognizable, his skin blue and his eyes sunken. John died that night, and Elizabeth, left with two young children and no means of support, was forced to rely on the charity of neighbors equally stricken by the disease.

Grim Scenes in Hospitals and Streets

Hospitals, already overcrowded and understaffed, were pushed to the breaking point by the influx of cholera patients. In London's hospitals, the scenes were grim. Wards overflowed with the sick, their beds lined up side by side, with no space between them. The smell of death and disease permeated the air. Doctors and nurses, overwhelmed and exhausted, did their best to provide care, but there was little they could do. Most patients died within a day or two of being admitted, their bodies swiftly removed to make way for the next unfortunate victim.

On the streets, the situation was no better. In areas like Soho, one of the hardest-hit neighborhoods, the sight of bodies being loaded onto carts became a daily occurrence. The dead were often left outside their homes, wrapped in whatever cloth could be spared, awaiting collection. Burial grounds were filled to capacity, and the city's gravediggers could not keep up with the demand. The atmosphere was one of dread and desolation, with fear gripping the hearts of Londoners who saw no end in sight to the epidemic.

The disease's impact was not confined to the poorest districts. In more affluent neighborhoods, residents barricaded themselves in their homes, hoping to avoid contact with the infected. Even the wealthy, who had the means to flee the city, were not immune. The disease spread wherever contaminated water could reach, sparing no one. The pervasive fear and uncertainty about how the disease was transmitted led to widespread paranoia and suspicion.

A Pivotal Moment: John Snow's Findings

In the midst of this chaos, one man would emerge with a revolutionary idea that would challenge the prevailing miasma theory and change the course of public health forever. John Snow, a physician who had long questioned the established views on disease transmission, believed that cholera was not spread by "bad air" but by contaminated water. His ideas were initially met with skepticism and ridicule from the medical establishment, but Snow was undeterred.

Snow's opportunity to prove his theory came during the outbreak in Soho in 1854. He began a meticulous investigation, mapping the cases of cholera and interviewing affected families. His work led him to a seemingly innocuous public water pump on Broad Street, which was heavily used by the local residents. Through his interviews, Snow discovered that nearly all the victims had drawn water from this pump. In contrast, a nearby brewery, where workers drank only beer or water from a private well, had few cases of cholera.

Snow's breakthrough came when he had the pump's water tested. The results showed clear evidence of contamination, likely from a nearby cesspool that had leaked into the well. Armed with this evidence, Snow took his findings to the local authorities and persuaded them to remove the pump's handle, effectively shutting it down. Almost immediately, the number of new cholera cases in the area began to decline, providing dramatic support for Snow's theory that cholera was a waterborne disease.

Changing Public Health Understanding and Policy

Snow's findings, while groundbreaking, were not immediately accepted by the medical community or the general public. The miasma theory was deeply entrenched, and many were reluctant to abandon it. However, Snow's work marked the beginning of a shift in public health understanding and policy. Slowly, the evidence began to mount that cholera was indeed spread through contaminated water, not foul air.

In 1855, Snow presented his findings to the British government, advocating for a new approach to disease prevention that focused on sanitation and clean water supply. Although his ideas were initially met with resistance, they began to gain traction as more evidence emerged to support them. The realization that cholera could be prevented by improving water quality and sanitation led to the development of modern public health measures, including the construction of new sewage systems and the regulation of water supplies.

The Aftermath and Legacy

The Third Cholera Pandemic eventually waned, but its impact was felt long after the last case had disappeared. The pandemic exposed the vulnerabilities of rapidly growing industrial cities and highlighted the need for better urban planning and public health infrastructure. It also marked a turning point in the understanding of disease transmission, paving the way for the germ theory of disease, which would revolutionize medicine in the years to come.

The work of John Snow, once dismissed by his contemporaries, would come to be recognized as a pioneering contribution to epidemiology and public health. His methods of mapping disease outbreaks and using statistical analysis to identify sources of infection laid the groundwork for future public health investigations. Snow's findings helped to shift the focus from treating disease to preventing it, a shift that would save countless lives in the years to come.

Reflections on Fear, Confusion, and Progress

The Third Cholera Pandemic was a period of immense suffering and fear, but it was also a time of critical learning and progress. The confusion and terror that gripped cities across the world were born from a lack of understanding, but out of that darkness came a new era of public health. The lessons learned during this pandemic would prove invaluable in the fight against future outbreaks, as cities and nations sought to build healthier, more resilient communities.

As we reflect on this chapter of history, we are reminded of the importance of scientific inquiry, open-mindedness, and perseverance in the face of adversity. The story of the Third Cholera Pandemic is not just one of tragedy, but also of discovery and progress, a testament to humanity's capacity to learn, adapt, and overcome even the most fearsome challenges.

Part 8: The Russian Flu (1889-1890)

In the late 19th century, the world was on the cusp of a new era. Technological advancements in transportation and communication were shrinking distances, bringing nations closer together in trade, culture, and diplomacy. Yet, this growing interconnectedness also had a darker side—one that became all too apparent in the winter of 1889, when an unfamiliar and deadly enemy began to spread across Europe. This was the Russian Flu, the first modern flu pandemic, a disease that would bring death and fear to the rapidly industrializing world and serve as a stark reminder of the vulnerabilities that came with progress.

The First Signs: A Dismissed Threat

The first reports of a strange new illness came in late 1889, from the steppes of Central Asia and the Russian Empire. In the city of Bukhara, deep in the heart of Central Asia, physicians noticed an uptick in cases of what seemed to be a particularly severe form of influenza. Patients presented with sudden high fevers, severe headaches, muscle pains, and a persistent cough. Most concerning, however, was how quickly the disease seemed to spread from person to person. Within weeks, entire households and villages were stricken.

Yet, these initial warnings went largely unnoticed by the broader world. Influenza was a familiar foe, a disease that had made regular appearances throughout history, often striking in waves during the colder months. Local officials, assuming this was just another seasonal outbreak, took little action beyond advising the sick to stay home and rest. Life continued as usual in the bustling streets and bazaars of Bukhara and other nearby cities.

But as winter deepened, the flu did not subside. Instead, it seemed to gather strength, spreading northward and westward, following the paths of trade and migration. By early November, cases were being reported in the Russian capital of St. Petersburg. The city, a hub of commerce and culture, was unprepared for what was to come. As the days grew colder, the flu's grip tightened. The city's doctors, accustomed to dealing with the usual winter maladies, were overwhelmed by the sheer number of patients filling their clinics and hospitals.

The Rapid Escalation

By December 1889, it was clear that this was no ordinary flu. Reports of a mysterious and deadly "Russian influenza" began to appear in newspapers across Europe. The disease had spread rapidly from St. Petersburg, moving westward along the railways and trade routes that connected the Russian Empire with the rest of Europe. In Berlin, Paris, and Vienna, cases multiplied with alarming speed. The disease seemed to have an insatiable appetite, infecting people of all ages and backgrounds, sparing no one.

In London, the news of the "Russian Flu" was initially met with skepticism. The British press, confident in the superiority of their public health system, downplayed the threat. They dismissed the reports from Russia as exaggerated or unreliable, a consequence of the poor sanitation and hygiene of the Tsarist Empire. But within weeks, the first cases appeared in London's crowded East End. The virus moved swiftly through the city's dense neighborhoods, its victims struck down with fever, fatigue, and a relentless cough that seemed to tear through the lungs.

As the number of cases grew, so did the fear. The British government, initially complacent, scrambled to respond. Hospitals were quickly overwhelmed, and the city's public health officials were at a loss. The traditional remedies for influenza—rest, warm fluids, and poultices—seemed to have little effect against this new, more virulent strain. The death toll began to rise, and with it, the sense of dread. This was not the influenza they knew. This was something far more deadly.

A Growing Realization: A Pandemic Unfolds

As the flu spread across Europe, the realization began to dawn on populations and governments alike: this was not an ordinary influenza outbreak. This was a pandemic. In city after city, the story was the same—hospitals filled beyond capacity, doctors and nurses overwhelmed, and death rates climbing. In Paris, where the disease arrived just before Christmas, the mood was one of both disbelief and terror. The city, known for its joie de vivre, now seemed haunted by the specter of death. The great boulevards, usually filled with the bustle of life, were eerily quiet as people stayed indoors, afraid to venture out into the cold, infected air.

In Berlin, the German government declared a state of emergency as the number of cases soared. The city's hospitals, already stretched thin, began to run out of beds, and temporary facilities were set up in schools and churches to accommodate the overflow of patients. The streets, once vibrant with the energy of a rapidly modernizing capital, were now filled with the somber processions of funeral carts carrying the dead to hastily dug graves. The fear and uncertainty were palpable. The Russian Flu was unlike any flu seen before. It spread faster, struck harder, and killed more.

Even in the United States, thousands of miles away, the news from Europe caused alarm. American newspapers followed the spread of the flu closely, publishing daily updates on the rising death tolls in Europe's major cities. By January 1890, the flu had crossed the Atlantic, arriving in New York City. The disease spread quickly through the city's immigrant neighborhoods, where overcrowding and poor sanitation provided fertile ground for its deadly advance.

Suspense and Fear: A Society on Edge

As the pandemic progressed, the atmosphere across Europe and beyond grew increasingly tense and fearful. People began to dread the slightest cough or sneeze, worried that it might be the first sign of infection. Schools closed, businesses shuttered, and theaters went dark as public gatherings were discouraged or outright banned. In many places, the fear of contagion led to social isolation, with families barricading themselves in their homes and avoiding all contact with the outside world.

The uncertainty of the situation only added to the fear. Little was understood about how the flu spread, and theories abounded. Some believed it was transmitted through foul air or "miasmas," while others speculated about the role of cold weather or personal hygiene. There were even those who claimed it was a punishment from God for the sins of the modern age. With no clear understanding of the disease's transmission, people grasped for any explanation that might make sense of the unfolding disaster.

In Vienna, a city renowned for its intellectual and artistic life, the flu struck down many of the city's most prominent figures. The famed composer Johann Strauss II, known as the "Waltz King," fell ill with the flu but managed to survive. Others were not so fortunate. The city's artistic and literary circles were decimated, and the cultural life of the city ground to a halt. The cafes, once filled with lively debate and discussion, were now empty and silent, the patrons too afraid to gather in public spaces.

Personal Accounts: Stories of Loss and Survival

Amidst the horror of the Russian Flu, personal stories of loss and survival emerged, capturing the human dimension of the pandemic. In St. Petersburg, the disease's first European foothold, a young factory worker named Dmitri watched in horror as his fellow workers fell ill one by one. The factory floor, usually bustling with the noise of machinery and labor, became a place of deathly silence as more and more workers were sent home or to the hospital, never to return.

Dmitri's own family was not spared. His wife, Anna, succumbed to the flu after a brief but brutal illness, leaving him to care for their two small children. Overwhelmed with grief and fear, Dmitri struggled to keep his family safe in a city ravaged by disease. Every day, he walked to work, his heart heavy with dread, wondering if this would be the day he, too, would fall victim to the invisible killer.

In New York, a young nurse named Clara worked tirelessly in one of the city's overcrowded hospitals. She had come to the city from Ireland, hoping for a new life and opportunity, but now found herself in the midst of a crisis she could never have imagined. The hospital wards were filled with the sick and dying, their faces pale and drawn, their bodies racked with fever. Clara, exhausted but determined, moved from bed to bed, administering what care she could. She knew that for many, there was little she could do but offer comfort in their final hours. Yet she continued, driven by a sense of duty and compassion that refused to be extinguished by the darkness around her.

The Rise of Public Health Responses

As the death toll rose and the scale of the pandemic became clear, governments and public health officials around the world began to take more decisive action. In London, the newly formed Metropolitan Board of Works initiated a series of measures aimed at controlling the spread of the flu. Public health campaigns were launched to educate the public about the importance of hygiene and sanitation, and efforts were made to improve the city's water supply and waste disposal systems.

In Paris, the French government ordered the closure of public spaces and implemented quarantines in an attempt to stem the tide of infection. The city's hospitals were expanded, and new facilities were built to accommodate the growing number of patients. In Berlin, the German government established a network of fever clinics to provide care to those affected and prevent the spread of the disease.

These measures, while necessary, often proved insufficient against the virulence of the Russian Flu. The disease continued to spread, and the death toll continued to climb. The sense of helplessness and frustration grew, as people realized that their governments, despite their best efforts, could not protect them from the invisible enemy that seemed to be everywhere and nowhere at once.

A Global Pandemic: The Toll and the Aftermath

By the time the Russian Flu began to wane in the spring of 1890, it had claimed the lives of an estimated one million people worldwide. The pandemic had spread to every continent, leaving a trail of death and despair in its wake. In the industrialized cities of Europe and North America, the toll was particularly heavy, with dense populations and crowded living conditions providing ideal conditions for the virus to spread.

The pandemic had a profound impact on public health policy and medical research. The experience of the Russian Flu highlighted the need for better understanding of infectious diseases and their transmission. It spurred the development of new medical techniques and the establishment of public health institutions dedicated to disease prevention and control.

The Russian Flu also served as a stark reminder of the vulnerabilities that came with progress. The very networks that had brought the world closer together—railways, steamships, and telegraph lines—had also facilitated the rapid spread of disease. The pandemic forced a reckoning with the realities of a modern, interconnected world and underscored the importance of preparedness and vigilance in the face of emerging threats.

Reflections on the Russian Flu

The Russian Flu was a wake-up call to a rapidly changing world, a stark reminder of the fragility of human societies in the face of new and unpredictable threats. It was a disease that struck with unprecedented speed and ferocity, challenging the assumptions of the time and leaving a lasting mark on the societies it touched.

As we reflect on the Russian Flu, we are reminded of the importance of humility, adaptability, and resilience in the face of uncertainty. The lessons learned from this pandemic continue to resonate today, as we face new challenges in a world that remains interconnected and interdependent. The Russian Flu was not just a moment of fear and loss, but also a catalyst for change, a moment that spurred new thinking and new approaches to public health and disease prevention.

Part 9: The Spanish Flu (1918-1919)

The year was 1918. The world was weary, battered by four years of relentless warfare that had claimed millions of lives. World War I, the "War to End All Wars," was drawing to a close, and across Europe and beyond, a fragile peace was beginning to take shape. But just as the guns fell silent on the Western Front, a new and far more insidious enemy emerged—an enemy that would claim more lives than the war itself. This was the Spanish Flu, a pandemic of unprecedented scale and virulence that would sweep across the globe in three devastating waves, leaving a world already on its knees gasping for breath.

The First Wave: A Prelude to Disaster

The origins of the Spanish Flu remain a subject of debate among historians, but most agree that the first recorded cases appeared in the spring of 1918, among soldiers stationed at Fort Riley, Kansas, in the United States. Initially, the illness seemed mild, little more than a particularly bad strain of seasonal influenza. Soldiers experienced typical flu-like symptoms: fever, fatigue, sore throat, and body aches. While a few cases resulted in complications, the overall mortality rate appeared low, and most patients recovered after a few days of rest.

However, as soldiers traveled from the U.S. to Europe to join the ongoing war effort, the disease began to spread. By April, cases were being reported in military camps across France, and soon after, in the civilian population. The initial response was one of cautious concern rather than alarm. In the context of a world still at war, a new strain of flu seemed a minor concern. Yet, beneath this veneer of complacency, the virus was mutating, becoming more virulent and preparing to strike again with far deadlier force.

By the summer of 1918, the first wave of the flu seemed to be subsiding, and attention turned back to the final months of the war. But the virus was far from done. It was merely waiting, adapting, and readying itself for what would come next.

The Second Wave: Death Comes Swiftly

In August 1918, the Spanish Flu returned with a vengeance. This time, the virus was different—stronger, deadlier, and more insidious. The second wave began in Boston, where cases quickly exploded among the city's dockworkers and military personnel. Within weeks, the disease had spread to cities across the eastern United States, and from there, it leapt back across the Atlantic, striking Europe with terrifying speed.

Unlike the first wave, the second wave of the Spanish Flu was marked by its extreme virulence and high mortality rate. The disease seemed to target young, healthy adults—those in the prime of life—rather than the very young and the elderly, as was typical of most flu strains. Victims often succumbed within days of the first symptoms, their lungs rapidly filling with fluid, leaving them gasping for air. The speed and severity of the disease caught everyone off guard.

In London, the flu hit hard and fast. Hospitals, already strained from years of war, were quickly overwhelmed. The city's doctors and nurses, exhausted and depleted from treating wounded soldiers, now found themselves facing a new, invisible enemy. The wards filled with patients, their faces blue from lack of oxygen, their bodies wracked with violent coughs. The air was thick with the sounds of suffering—the gasping breaths of the dying, the cries of those in pain, and the low murmurs of exhausted medical staff.

The rapid transmission of the virus created a sense of panic among the population. Public gatherings were banned, schools and theaters closed, and citizens were urged to stay indoors. The streets of London, usually bustling with activity, fell eerily silent as people retreated into their homes, hoping to avoid the deadly air outside.

Global Spread: A Pandemic in Motion

The Spanish Flu did not confine itself to Europe and North America. As quickly as it spread across the Atlantic, it moved to the rest of the world. In India, the pandemic struck with ferocious intensity. Cities like Bombay (now Mumbai) and Calcutta (now Kolkata) saw their populations decimated as the flu spread through crowded neighborhoods, trains, and markets. The disease overwhelmed the rudimentary public health infrastructure, and bodies piled up faster than they could be cremated or buried. The death toll in India alone is estimated to have reached 10-20 million, making it one of the hardest-hit regions in the world.

In South Africa, the flu arrived in September 1918, brought by a ship returning from Europe. Within weeks, the disease spread to the gold mining towns and rural areas, claiming thousands of lives. The lack of medical facilities and trained personnel exacerbated the crisis, and entire communities were wiped out. The impact on the economy was severe, as businesses shuttered and agricultural production ground to a halt.

In the Pacific, remote islands that had been relatively untouched by the war found themselves vulnerable to the disease. Samoa, for example, saw over a quarter of its population perish within a matter of months. The speed at which the flu spread across the globe, reaching even the most isolated regions, underscored the interconnectedness of the modern world and the vulnerabilities that came with it.

Suspense and Panic: A Society in Fear

As the flu continued to spread, the sense of panic deepened. In city after city, town after town, the story was the same: hospitals overwhelmed, bodies piling up, and a pervasive fear that gripped every corner of society. People began to dread the slightest cough or sneeze, worried that it might be the first sign of infection. The unpredictability of the disease—its ability to strike anyone, anywhere, at any time—created an atmosphere of suspense and dread.

In New York City, the streets were empty, save for the occasional ambulance racing to a hospital or a horse-drawn cart carrying away the dead. Shops were closed, and the usual hustle and bustle of the city was replaced by an eerie silence. The city's public health officials, overwhelmed by the scale of the crisis, issued directives urging people to wear masks and avoid public gatherings. Newspapers ran headlines daily, tracking the rising death toll and offering grim advice on how to avoid infection.

In San Francisco, the city's Board of Health mandated the wearing of gauze masks in public, declaring, "Obey the laws, and wear the gauze; protect your jaws from septic paws." The slogan, while catchy, did little to ease the fear that gripped the city. Citizens, desperate for any measure of protection, complied, but the masks provided little defense against a virus that spread so easily through the air.

The Overwhelming of Hospitals

The Spanish Flu overwhelmed hospitals and medical facilities around the world. In Paris, the wards were filled beyond capacity, with patients lying on stretchers in hallways and corridors. The city's doctors, many of whom were themselves suffering from the flu, worked around the clock, administering what care they could. Yet, there was little they could do against a disease that seemed to defy all known treatments.

In Philadelphia, one of the hardest-hit cities in the United States, the situation was dire. Hospitals were so overwhelmed that medical students were pressed into service to care for the sick. In some cases, patients were turned away, forced to return home to die. The city, which had held a massive Liberty Loan parade just weeks earlier, became a ghost town, its streets filled with the stench of death and decay. The decision to go ahead with the parade, against the advice of health officials, proved catastrophic, as it facilitated the rapid spread of the disease through the densely packed crowds.

Implementation of Public Health Measures

Faced with a rapidly spreading pandemic and no effective treatment, governments and public health officials were forced to take drastic measures to control the outbreak. Quarantines were implemented, and entire neighborhoods were cordoned off. Public gatherings were banned, and travel was restricted in an attempt to slow the spread of the virus. In some cities, schools and churches were converted into makeshift hospitals to accommodate the overflow of patients.

In Chicago, the city's health commissioner issued a directive to close all schools, theaters, and places of public amusement. Streetcars were ordered to run with windows open, regardless of the weather, in an effort to improve ventilation. In Boston, similar measures were taken, with public health officials instructing citizens to avoid crowded places and maintain good personal hygiene. Despite these efforts, the flu continued to spread, and the death toll continued to rise.

In rural areas, the situation was often worse. Lacking access to medical care and information, many communities were left to fend for themselves. Entire families succumbed to the disease, their bodies discovered only days or weeks later by neighbors or authorities. In some remote areas, there was no one left to bury the dead, and mass graves became a grim necessity.

Personal Accounts: Stories of Desperation and Courage

Amidst the chaos and death of the Spanish Flu, countless personal stories of desperation, loss, and courage emerged. In Madrid, where the flu had earned its name due to the extensive coverage by the Spanish press, a young mother named Isabella watched helplessly as her husband and two children fell ill. The hospitals were full, and there was no help to be found. She did what she could, caring for them at home with makeshift remedies and prayers. Her husband succumbed to the disease within days, leaving her alone to care for their children, who were too weak to cry. Against all odds, her youngest daughter survived, a small glimmer of hope in a city ravaged by death.

In a small village in Alaska, the flu arrived in the late fall of 1918, brought by a visiting trader. The disease spread quickly through the close-knit community, and within weeks, more than half of the population had died. An orphaned boy named Anook, only ten years old, was one of the few survivors. With no adults left to care for him, he and a handful of other children banded together, scavenging for food and doing their best to stay warm in the harsh winter cold. Their resilience in the face of unimaginable loss is a testament to the human spirit's capacity to endure.

The Eerie Silence After the Pandemic's End

By the summer of 1919, the Spanish Flu pandemic had largely run its course, leaving behind a world forever changed. An estimated 50 million people had died, though some estimates suggest the toll could have been as high as 100 million. The sheer scale of the pandemic was staggering, far surpassing the death toll of the recently concluded World War I. In many places, the toll of the flu was so great that it left behind a silence that was almost as unsettling as the disease itself.

In the towns and cities of Europe, North America, and beyond, life slowly began to return to normal. Schools reopened, businesses resumed operations, and people returned to the streets. But the scars left by the pandemic were deep. Many families had been shattered, losing multiple members in a matter of weeks. Entire communities had been decimated, their populations permanently reduced. The world, already traumatized by war, now had to grapple with the aftereffects of a pandemic that had reached every corner of the globe.

In the United States, the economic impact was significant, as industries that had been gearing up for peacetime production now faced a labor shortage due to the high mortality rate. In Europe, still reeling from the war, the pandemic exacerbated existing social and economic challenges. The loss of so many young adults—those who would have been the driving force behind post-war reconstruction—added to the sense of uncertainty and instability.

Reflections on the Spanish Flu

The Spanish Flu remains one of the most devastating pandemics in human history, a stark reminder of the fragility of life and the vulnerabilities of even the most advanced societies. It was a pandemic that struck with unprecedented speed and ferocity, leaving a world already scarred by war reeling from a new and unexpected threat. Yet, it also spurred significant advances in public health and medical science, as governments and health organizations recognized the need for better preparedness and response to future pandemics.

The Spanish Flu highlighted the importance of international cooperation and the need for robust public health infrastructure. It underscored the critical role of science and research in understanding and combating infectious diseases and laid the groundwork for future efforts to prevent and control pandemics. The lessons learned from the Spanish Flu would prove invaluable in the fight against subsequent outbreaks, as the world sought to build a more resilient and prepared global community.

As we reflect on the Spanish Flu, we are reminded of the strength and resilience of the human spirit in the face of unimaginable adversity. The stories of loss, courage, and survival that emerged from this dark chapter in history are a testament to our collective capacity to endure and overcome. The Spanish Flu was not just a moment of unprecedented tragedy but also a catalyst for change, a moment that reshaped the world and set the stage for a new era of public health and global cooperation.

Part 10: The HIV/AIDS Epidemic (1980s-Present)

The early 1980s was a time of dynamic change and optimism. Advances in technology, medicine, and culture had brought about a new era of progress and possibility. Yet, amidst this backdrop of hope, a new and mysterious disease began to emerge, one that would come to define a generation and challenge the world in ways that few could have imagined. This was the HIV/AIDS epidemic, a crisis that would spread across the globe, bringing with it fear, stigma, and an ongoing struggle for understanding, compassion, and effective treatment.

The First Signs: A Medical Mystery Unfolds

The first documented cases of what would later become known as AIDS (Acquired Immune Deficiency Syndrome) appeared in the United States in 1981. Physicians in New York and California began noticing a troubling trend among young, previously healthy gay men who were presenting with rare infections and cancers—conditions typically seen only in patients with severely compromised immune systems. These conditions included Pneumocystis pneumonia (PCP), a fungal infection of the lungs, and Kaposi's sarcoma, a rare form of cancer that caused dark lesions on the skin and internal organs.

At first, these cases were few, isolated, and confined to specific communities. But as more and more young men fell ill, doctors realized that they were facing something unprecedented. The patients' immune systems appeared to be inexplicably failing, leaving them vulnerable to infections and cancers that their bodies would normally be able to fight off. The disease progressed rapidly, and within months, many of the patients were dead.

Medical professionals were baffled. The Centers for Disease Control and Prevention (CDC) issued a report in June 1981 that described the unusual cluster of cases but could offer no explanation for their cause. The disease seemed to strike out of nowhere, with no clear pattern or origin. This lack of understanding only heightened the sense of mystery and fear surrounding the emerging epidemic.

The Fear and Stigma Take Hold

As the number of cases grew, so did the fear. The disease, which initially seemed to affect primarily gay men, was quickly labeled by the media as the "gay plague." This label not only stigmatized those affected but also contributed to a widespread sense of panic and misinformation. The lack of knowledge about how the disease was transmitted led to irrational fears and speculation. Was it airborne? Was it transmitted through casual contact? The uncertainty fueled fear, discrimination, and prejudice.

The gay community, already marginalized and facing widespread social stigma, found itself at the epicenter of a burgeoning public health crisis. The disease became a focal point for deep-seated prejudices and societal anxieties about sexuality, morality, and public health. In many parts of the world, those who were infected faced not just a deadly illness, but also intense social ostracism and discrimination.

Yet, even as fear and stigma took hold, there were those who sought to challenge the prevailing narratives and fight back. In San Francisco, New York, and other major cities, gay rights activists began to organize, demanding attention, resources, and respect for those affected by the disease. This activism was born out of necessity, as many within the community watched their friends and loved ones fall ill and die, often with little understanding or support from the broader public or the government.

Personal Stories: The Human Cost of the Epidemic

Amidst the growing panic and confusion, countless personal stories began to emerge, each highlighting the profound human cost of the epidemic. In New York City, a young artist named David struggled to make sense of the disease that was ravaging his community. David had come to New York in the late 1970s, drawn by the city's vibrant arts scene and the promise of freedom. But by 1982, many of his closest friends were dead or dying, their bodies wasting away from a disease that no one seemed to understand.

David's own diagnosis came in 1983, a year after his partner, Michael, had succumbed to the disease. The news was devastating, but David refused to give in to despair. He began documenting his experiences through a series of paintings and writings, capturing the pain, fear, and confusion that had come to define his life. His work, raw and emotional, provided a powerful commentary on the epidemic and became a voice for those who felt abandoned and forgotten.

In San Francisco, a nurse named Mary found herself on the front lines of the crisis. Working at a public hospital, she saw firsthand the toll that the disease was taking on her city. Her ward, once filled with a diverse array of patients, was now almost entirely devoted to those suffering from AIDS-related illnesses. Mary became a fierce advocate for her patients, many of whom were shunned by their families and left to die alone. She fought for better care, more funding, and greater compassion from the public and the medical community.

The Activism That Arose

As the epidemic continued to spread, so too did the activism that arose in response. Groups like the Gay Men's Health Crisis (GMHC) and the AIDS Coalition to Unleash Power (ACT UP) emerged, fighting for better research, more funding, and fair treatment for those affected. These organizations became powerful voices in the struggle against AIDS, challenging both the public's perception of the disease and the government's often lackluster response.

In 1987, ACT UP was founded in New York City by a group of activists, including playwright and author Larry Kramer, who were frustrated by the lack of action and urgency in the fight against AIDS. ACT UP quickly became known for its direct-action tactics and confrontational style. The group staged protests at government buildings, pharmaceutical companies, and even the offices of major newspapers, demanding more funding for AIDS research, faster approval of new drugs, and an end to discrimination against those living with HIV/AIDS.

One of ACT UP's most famous actions took place in 1989, when members of the group staged a "die-in" at St. Patrick's Cathedral in New York City to protest the Catholic Church's stance on condom use and its opposition to safer sex education. The demonstration, which involved hundreds of activists lying down in the aisles of the cathedral, drew national attention and highlighted the desperate need for more comprehensive public health measures.

The Struggle for Understanding and Treatment

Despite the growing activism and awareness, the early years of the HIV/AIDS epidemic were marked by confusion, fear, and a lack of effective treatment. The disease, initially identified as a mysterious new form of immune deficiency, was not well understood, and there was no cure. Early efforts to develop a treatment were hampered by limited funding, bureaucratic hurdles, and the stigma associated with the disease.

It wasn't until 1983 that scientists identified the virus responsible for AIDS: the Human Immunodeficiency Virus (HIV). This discovery was a critical step forward in understanding the disease, but it was just the beginning of a long and difficult journey toward treatment. Researchers faced immense challenges in developing effective therapies for HIV, which was found to mutate rapidly and attack the very cells designed to defend the body.

The first breakthrough came in 1987 with the approval of AZT (zidovudine), the first antiretroviral drug for the treatment of HIV. AZT was initially hailed as a potential "miracle drug," but its high cost and severe side effects limited its effectiveness. For many, AZT was a harsh reminder of how far there was still to go in the fight against AIDS.

Meanwhile, the epidemic continued to spread. By the late 1980s, it was clear that HIV/AIDS was not confined to any one community or country. The disease had spread to every corner of the globe, affecting people of all races, genders, and sexual orientations. In sub-Saharan Africa, the epidemic was particularly devastating, with entire communities and even countries grappling with the enormous social, economic, and public health impacts of the disease.

Ongoing Struggles and Breakthroughs

As the epidemic moved into the 1990s, the fight against HIV/AIDS became increasingly global. International organizations, governments, and non-profits worked to address the spread of the virus and the growing humanitarian crisis. In 1996, the introduction of highly active antiretroviral therapy (HAART) marked a turning point in the treatment of HIV. This combination therapy, which used multiple antiretroviral drugs to suppress the virus, dramatically improved the prognosis for those living with HIV, turning what had once been a death sentence into a manageable chronic condition for many.

Yet, despite these advancements, significant challenges remained. Access to treatment was uneven, with many low-income countries struggling to afford the costly medications. Stigma and discrimination persisted, fueled by misinformation and prejudice. In many places, those living with HIV/AIDS were still ostracized, denied employment, or subjected to violence and abuse.

The ongoing struggle to overcome these challenges inspired a new wave of activism and advocacy. In South Africa, where the government was slow to respond to the epidemic, grassroots organizations like the Treatment Action Campaign (TAC) emerged, fighting for access to life-saving medications and greater awareness of HIV prevention. TAC's efforts, which included protests, legal challenges, and public education campaigns, played a crucial role in shifting public policy and increasing access to treatment in one of the world's hardest-hit countries.

Personal Stories of Resilience and Advocacy

The fight against HIV/AIDS has been marked by countless stories of resilience, courage, and advocacy. In Zimbabwe, a young woman named Prudence, who was diagnosed with HIV in the late 1990s, became a powerful voice for those living with the disease. Despite facing intense stigma and discrimination, Prudence used her story to educate others about HIV and to advocate for better treatment and support for those affected. Her efforts helped to challenge the silence and denial that surrounded the epidemic in her community and inspired others to speak out.

In the United States, Ryan White, a teenage hemophiliac who contracted HIV through a contaminated blood transfusion, became a symbol of the fight against AIDS-related stigma. Ryan's story, which drew national attention in the mid-1980s, highlighted the prejudice faced by those living with HIV, even among children. Ryan and his mother, Jeanne, became tireless advocates for HIV education and research, helping to shift public perception of the disease and pave the way for greater understanding and acceptance.

The Global Fight Continues

As the 21st century dawned, the fight against HIV/AIDS continued on a global scale. The epidemic, which had already claimed millions of lives, remained a major public health crisis, particularly in sub-Saharan Africa, where infection rates were highest. International efforts, including the establishment of the Global Fund to Fight AIDS, Tuberculosis, and Malaria and the U.S. President's Emergency Plan for AIDS Relief (PEPFAR), helped to expand access to treatment and prevention services in low-income countries.

These efforts, coupled with advances in medical research, have led to significant progress in the fight against HIV/AIDS. The development of pre-exposure prophylaxis (PrEP), a medication that can prevent HIV infection, has provided a new tool for preventing the spread of the virus. Efforts to reduce mother-to-child transmission have also been successful, resulting in a significant decline in new infections among newborns.

Yet, despite these gains, challenges remain. In many parts of the world, stigma, discrimination, and lack of access to healthcare continue to hinder efforts to combat the epidemic. The emergence of drug-resistant strains of HIV poses a new threat, and the need for a vaccine remains urgent.

Reflections on the HIV/AIDS Epidemic

The HIV/AIDS epidemic is one of the most significant public health challenges of the modern era, a crisis that has reshaped societies, challenged scientific understanding, and tested the limits of compassion and empathy. It is a story of fear and stigma, but also of resilience, advocacy, and progress. The fight against HIV/AIDS has brought out the best and worst in humanity, highlighting both the capacity for cruelty and indifference, and the power of community, activism, and solidarity.

As we reflect on the HIV/AIDS epidemic, we are reminded of the importance of education, empathy, and action in the face of crisis. The lessons learned from this ongoing struggle continue to inform efforts to combat other global health challenges and underscore the need for a comprehensive, compassionate, and science-based approach to public health.

The fight against HIV/AIDS is far from over, but the progress made in the past four decades offers hope for a future where the epidemic is finally brought under control. Until then, the stories of those who have fought, suffered, and survived will continue to inspire and guide us in the pursuit of a world free from the fear and devastation of HIV/AIDS.

Part 11: The SARS Pandemic (2002-2003)

In the early 21st century, the world was becoming increasingly interconnected. Advances in travel, communication, and technology had made it easier than ever for people, goods, and information to cross borders. Yet, this global interconnectedness also brought new challenges—challenges that became frighteningly clear in late 2002 when a mysterious illness began to spread in southern China. This illness would come to be known as Severe Acute Respiratory Syndrome, or SARS, and its sudden emergence would spark a global panic, a frantic race against time to identify and contain the virus, and a dramatic reminder of the vulnerabilities that come with living in a connected world.

The First Cases: A Mystery in Guangdong

The first known cases of SARS appeared in November 2002 in Guangdong Province, a densely populated region in southern China known for its vibrant markets and bustling cities. Patients presented with symptoms that were initially mistaken for atypical pneumonia: high fever, chills, muscle aches, and a dry cough. However, unlike typical pneumonia, this illness was highly contagious and quickly spread among hospital staff and family members caring for the sick.

Local doctors were baffled by the new disease, which seemed to spread with alarming ease. Within weeks, several hospitals in Guangdong were overwhelmed with cases. As the number of patients grew, so did the fear among healthcare workers and the general public. The disease was unlike anything they had seen before, and there were no effective treatments. By early 2003, it became clear that this was no ordinary outbreak.

Despite the growing number of cases, information about the new illness was slow to reach the outside world. The Chinese government, wary of causing public panic and mindful of the potential economic impact, initially downplayed the severity of the situation. Local media coverage was limited, and health officials were discouraged from sharing information with international counterparts. This secrecy would prove costly, as the virus continued to spread, unknowingly carried by travelers moving between cities and across borders.

The Sudden Spread: From China to the World

The SARS virus, later identified as a novel coronavirus, spread rapidly from Guangdong to other parts of China and beyond. By February 2003, cases were being reported in Hong Kong, a major international hub. The virus entered Hong Kong through a single infected doctor from Guangdong, who checked into the Metropole Hotel. During his stay, the doctor, unaware he was carrying a highly contagious virus, infected several other guests staying on the same floor. These guests, in turn, carried the virus to their home countries, unknowingly setting off a chain reaction that would send SARS around the world.

Within days, SARS had spread to Vietnam, Singapore, Canada, and other countries, carried by international travelers who showed no symptoms at the time of their journeys. The virus seemed to move with a deadly precision, striking without warning and spreading with a speed that caught health officials off guard. In hospitals in Hanoi, Toronto, and Singapore, the first patients began to appear, their symptoms mirroring those seen in Guangdong and Hong Kong: high fever, respiratory distress, and, in severe cases, organ failure.

The sudden emergence of SARS on the global stage set off alarm bells at the World Health Organization (WHO) and other international health agencies. The WHO quickly issued a global alert, warning of the potential for a major international outbreak. In the halls of government and health agencies around the world, a sense of urgency and fear took hold. This was a new and unknown pathogen, and it was spreading fast.

Race Against Time: Identifying the Virus

As the number of SARS cases continued to rise, scientists and health officials around the world began a frantic race against time to identify the virus and understand how it was transmitted. The challenge was immense. SARS was a new disease, and little was known about its origins, its mode of transmission, or how to effectively treat it. The only certainty was that it was highly contagious and potentially deadly.

Laboratories across the globe worked around the clock, collaborating in an unprecedented international effort to identify the causative agent. In late March 2003, a team of researchers at the University of Hong Kong, led by microbiologist Malik Peiris, isolated a novel coronavirus from a patient's lung tissue. This discovery was a critical breakthrough, providing the first concrete evidence that SARS was caused by a new strain of coronavirus—a family of viruses known to cause respiratory illnesses in humans and animals.

Identifying the virus was only the first step. Researchers quickly turned their attention to understanding how SARS spread and how it could be contained. Early evidence suggested that the virus was primarily transmitted through respiratory droplets, but there were also indications that it could spread through contact with contaminated surfaces and, in some cases, through the air. This uncertainty added to the fear and confusion surrounding the outbreak, making it difficult for health officials to develop effective containment strategies.

Dramatic Quarantines and Travel Restrictions

With the virus spreading rapidly and no effective treatment in sight, governments and health agencies turned to the only tool they had left: containment. Quarantines were imposed in affected areas, and travel restrictions were put in place to prevent the spread of the virus. In Hong Kong, entire apartment complexes were sealed off after residents were found to be infected. In Singapore, hundreds of people were placed under quarantine, their movements monitored to prevent further transmission.

In Toronto, which quickly became the epicenter of the outbreak in North America, public health officials declared a state of emergency. Hospitals were overwhelmed with patients, and healthcare workers were falling ill at an alarming rate. The city's authorities imposed strict quarantine measures, closing schools, canceling public events, and advising residents to avoid non-essential travel. The normally bustling streets of Toronto fell silent, a stark reminder of the fear and uncertainty that gripped the city.

The economic impact of these measures was severe. Businesses shuttered, tourism ground to a halt, and stock markets plunged as the world braced for a potential global pandemic. Airlines canceled flights, and travelers were subjected to rigorous screenings and health checks. The fear of SARS became pervasive, affecting not just those in the hardest-hit regions but also those thousands of miles away who worried that the virus could strike anywhere, at any time.

Personal Stories: Fear and Resilience in the Face of SARS

Amidst the global panic, personal stories of fear, loss, and resilience began to emerge. In Hong Kong, a nurse named Li Mei found herself on the front lines of the outbreak. As the virus spread through the city's hospitals, Li Mei worked long hours, caring for patients who were often terrified and alone. Many of her colleagues fell ill, and the fear of becoming infected weighed heavily on her mind. Yet, despite the risks, she continued to work, driven by a sense of duty and compassion for those in her care.

In Toronto, a firefighter named John watched in horror as the virus spread through his community. John's station was called to several SARS-related emergencies, and he and his fellow firefighters took every precaution to avoid becoming infected. But despite their efforts, one of John's closest friends and colleagues contracted the virus and died within days. John, grappling with the loss, channeled his grief into action, volunteering to help transport patients and provide support to overwhelmed healthcare workers.

In Singapore, a young doctor named Tan faced the difficult decision of whether to continue working in a hospital overwhelmed by SARS cases or to protect his family by staying away. Tan's wife was pregnant, and the thought of bringing the virus home terrified him. Yet, like so many others, he chose to stay, working tirelessly to save lives while taking every precaution to keep his family safe.

Containment Achieved: Relief and Caution

By the summer of 2003, it became clear that the global response to SARS had succeeded in containing the outbreak. The number of new cases began to decline, and the spread of the virus was largely halted. This success was due in large part to the swift and coordinated efforts of governments, health agencies, and medical professionals around the world, who implemented strict containment measures, developed rapid diagnostic tests, and shared critical information and resources.

The containment of SARS was a significant achievement, but it was not without its costs. The pandemic had claimed nearly 800 lives and infected over 8,000 people in more than two dozen countries. The economic impact was also profound, with billions of dollars in lost productivity, trade, and tourism. But perhaps the most lasting impact was the psychological toll—the fear, anxiety, and uncertainty that lingered even after the virus was brought under control.

In many places, life began to return to normal, but there was a sense of caution and vigilance that remained. In Hong Kong, the city's residents, who had endured months of fear and isolation, slowly began to venture out again. Schools and businesses reopened, and the city's streets filled with people once more. Yet, there was a lingering sense of unease—a recognition that the threat had not been entirely eliminated, that the world had only narrowly averted a far worse disaster.

The Legacy of SARS: A New Era of Global Health Preparedness

The SARS pandemic of 2002-2003 marked a turning point in global public health preparedness. The swift and coordinated response to the outbreak demonstrated the importance of international cooperation in combating emerging infectious diseases. The experience of SARS highlighted the need for rapid communication, transparent reporting, and collaboration among nations, public health agencies, and researchers.

In the wake of SARS, the World Health Organization and other international bodies implemented new protocols and guidelines to improve global response to future outbreaks. The International Health Regulations (IHR), revised in 2005, established a framework for reporting and responding to public health emergencies of international concern. These regulations were designed to ensure that outbreaks like SARS would be detected earlier and contained more effectively in the future.

SARS also spurred advances in virology and infectious disease research. Scientists developed new diagnostic tools and antiviral treatments, and there was a renewed focus on understanding the origins and transmission of coronaviruses. The lessons learned from SARS would prove invaluable in the fight against future outbreaks, including the Middle East Respiratory Syndrome (MERS) and the COVID-19 pandemic.

Reflections on SARS: A Cautionary Tale

The SARS pandemic serves as a cautionary tale about the vulnerabilities of a globalized world. It was a stark reminder that in an interconnected world, a new and unknown virus can spread rapidly, crossing borders and continents in a matter of days. The experience of SARS underscored the importance of vigilance, preparedness, and cooperation in the face of emerging infectious diseases.

As we reflect on the SARS pandemic, we are reminded of the speed at which the world responded to a new and unknown threat, the sacrifices made by healthcare workers and first responders, and the resilience of communities around the globe. The success in containing SARS was a testament to the power of science, collaboration, and the human spirit. Yet, it also served as a warning: that the fight against infectious diseases is far from over, and that we must remain vigilant, prepared, and united in our efforts to protect global health.

Part 12: The H1N1 Influenza Pandemic (2009-2010)

In the spring of 2009, as the world seemed to be moving past the shadows of recent economic crises and into a new era of recovery and hope, an unexpected threat emerged from an unlikely place. A new strain of influenza, H1N1, appeared seemingly out of nowhere, quickly spreading across borders and oceans. The H1N1 influenza pandemic, also known as the "swine flu," would become a stark reminder of the unpredictable nature of pandemics, the challenges of global health preparedness, and the mixed reactions of governments and the public when faced with an invisible enemy.

The First Signs: An Unfamiliar Threat from Mexico

In March 2009, health officials in Mexico began noticing an unusual surge in cases of respiratory illness. Patients exhibited symptoms similar to those of seasonal flu—fever, cough, sore throat, and body aches—but the illness seemed to be affecting younger, healthier people, a demographic usually less susceptible to severe complications from the flu. The cases were concentrated in Mexico City, a sprawling metropolis with millions of residents living in close quarters, ideal conditions for the spread of a respiratory virus.

Initially, the Mexican health authorities believed they were dealing with a particularly severe outbreak of seasonal influenza. However, as more cases emerged, it became clear that this was something new. Many patients developed severe pneumonia and respiratory distress, and the death toll began to rise. Concern turned to alarm as the virus spread beyond the initial outbreak zone, crossing state borders and reaching other cities across the country.

By late April, the World Health Organization (WHO) had been alerted to the emerging situation in Mexico. The rapid spread of the illness, coupled with its unusual epidemiological profile, prompted an urgent investigation. Samples from infected patients were sent to laboratories around the world, where virologists worked around the clock to identify the pathogen. What they discovered was startling: a novel strain of H1N1 influenza, a mix of human, avian, and swine flu viruses that had never been seen before. This was a new and unknown strain of flu, and it was spreading fast.

The Rapid Spread: A Virus on the Move

The revelation that a novel H1N1 virus was responsible for the outbreak in Mexico sent shockwaves through the global health community. Influenza viruses are notoriously unpredictable and have a history of causing pandemics with devastating consequences. The fact that this new strain was spreading quickly and affecting younger people added to the urgency and concern. Within days of the WHO's announcement, cases of H1N1 began to surface in the United States, Canada, and several other countries, likely spread by travelers who had recently visited Mexico.

By early May, the virus had reached Europe, Asia, and Oceania. It spread with remarkable speed, facilitated by international air travel and the interconnectedness of modern societies. Airports became points of entry for the virus, with infected passengers unknowingly carrying it to new destinations. The flu spread from one continent to another in a matter of weeks, highlighting the vulnerabilities of a globalized world.

The rapid spread of H1N1 prompted countries around the world to implement emergency measures to try to contain the virus. Airports and border crossings instituted health screenings, looking for passengers with flu-like symptoms. Quarantines were imposed in some areas, and schools were closed in others. But despite these efforts, the virus continued to spread, moving faster than the containment measures could be implemented.

Public Reactions: Fear, Confusion, and Complacency

As news of the H1N1 virus spread, so too did fear and confusion. In Mexico, where the outbreak had begun, the streets of Mexico City, usually bustling with activity, fell eerily quiet as residents stayed indoors, fearful of contracting the virus. Schools and businesses were closed, and public gatherings were banned. The government urged citizens to wear masks and avoid unnecessary travel. The city took on the air of a ghost town, a place on edge, grappling with an invisible enemy.

Elsewhere, public reactions were mixed. In the United States, initial concern quickly gave way to a sense of complacency. The media dubbed the virus "swine flu," a term that linked it to pigs and gave the impression that the virus was primarily a problem for farmers and those in rural areas. The name, while catchy, was misleading. The virus was spreading among humans, not pigs, and its reach extended far beyond rural areas.

The mixed messages from health officials and the media contributed to confusion among the public. Some people dismissed the virus as overhyped, while others panicked, rushing to buy face masks and hand sanitizers. In some places, misinformation and rumors spread faster than the virus itself, leading to irrational fears and behaviors. In Egypt, for example, the government ordered the culling of all pigs in the country, despite there being no evidence that pigs in Egypt were infected or that such a measure would prevent human cases.

In Asia, the experience of the 2003 SARS outbreak influenced the public and government response. Countries like China, Singapore, and South Korea implemented strict quarantine measures and travel restrictions early on, hoping to contain the spread of the virus before it gained a foothold. In Japan, schools were closed, and public events were canceled. These actions, while effective in slowing the spread of the virus, also heightened public anxiety and fear.

The Global Scramble for Vaccines

As the H1N1 virus continued to spread, attention turned to the development of a vaccine. Influenza vaccines were nothing new; seasonal flu shots were already part of annual public health campaigns in many countries. However, creating a vaccine for a new strain like H1N1 posed unique challenges. Scientists needed to develop a vaccine that would be both safe and effective, and they needed to do it quickly.

The global scramble for vaccines was a race against time. Pharmaceutical companies ramped up production, and governments placed large orders, hoping to secure enough doses for their populations. The WHO worked with vaccine manufacturers, regulatory agencies, and public health organizations to accelerate the development and distribution process. Yet, despite these efforts, there were concerns about whether enough vaccine could be produced in time to prevent a severe pandemic.

In the United States, the Centers for Disease Control and Prevention (CDC) faced the daunting task of coordinating the distribution of millions of doses of the H1N1 vaccine. The challenge was compounded by the uncertainty surrounding the virus's behavior and the public's mixed reactions to vaccination campaigns. Many people were eager to get vaccinated, but there were also pockets of resistance, fueled by misinformation and distrust of vaccines.

In Europe, the situation was similar. Governments ordered millions of doses of the H1N1 vaccine, but logistical challenges and production delays meant that vaccines were not immediately available. Public health officials faced a difficult balancing act: managing public expectations, addressing fears and concerns about vaccine safety, and ensuring that those most at risk—such as healthcare workers, pregnant women, and those with underlying health conditions—were prioritized for vaccination.

Challenges Faced by Governments and Health Organizations

The H1N1 pandemic presented numerous challenges for governments and health organizations around the world. One of the most significant challenges was the need to communicate effectively with the public in an environment of uncertainty. The rapid spread of the virus, combined with the mixed messages from various sources, created a sense of confusion and fear. Public health officials had to walk a fine line between providing accurate information and avoiding unnecessary panic.

Another major challenge was the logistical complexity of distributing the vaccine on a global scale. The production of the H1N1 vaccine required significant resources and coordination among various stakeholders, including pharmaceutical companies, governments, and international organizations. Ensuring that vaccines were distributed equitably and efficiently was a daunting task, particularly given the logistical constraints and the urgency of the situation.

In many countries, healthcare systems were already stretched thin by the demands of seasonal flu and other illnesses. The addition of a new pandemic strain put further strain on hospitals, clinics, and public health infrastructure. Healthcare workers faced long hours, high-stress environments, and the constant risk of exposure to the virus. In some places, hospitals were overwhelmed, and temporary facilities were set up to accommodate the surge in patients.

Suspense and Uncertainty: The Pandemic's Unfolding

As the pandemic unfolded, the sense of suspense and uncertainty continued to grow. In city after city, country after country, the virus spread, affecting millions of people. Schools were closed, businesses shut down, and public events canceled. The world seemed to be holding its breath, waiting to see how the situation would evolve.

In Australia, where the flu season was just beginning as the virus spread, health officials braced for a potential surge in cases. The Australian government launched an aggressive vaccination campaign, aiming to inoculate as many people as possible before the virus could take hold. Despite these efforts, the virus spread rapidly, affecting tens of thousands and causing a significant number of deaths.

In South America, the virus spread through countries like Argentina, Brazil, and Chile, where the combination of winter weather and crowded urban centers provided ideal conditions for transmission. Public health officials in these countries faced the dual challenge of managing the pandemic while also addressing the ongoing needs of their populations, many of whom were already struggling with economic hardship and limited access to healthcare.

In Africa, where healthcare infrastructure was often limited and resources scarce, the spread of H1N1 posed a significant threat. The virus arrived in several countries, including South Africa, Kenya, and Nigeria, and while the number of cases was relatively low compared to other regions, the potential for a widespread outbreak was a major concern. International organizations, including the WHO and UNICEF, worked to provide support, including vaccines, medical supplies, and training for healthcare workers.

The Virus Slows: Relief and Reflection

By the early months of 2010, the H1N1 pandemic had begun to slow. The number of new cases decreased, and the virus seemed to be losing its momentum.

The rapid global response, including vaccination campaigns, public health measures, and increased awareness, had played a critical role in containing the spread of the virus and reducing its impact.

The relief was palpable, but there was also a sense of reflection. The pandemic had exposed both the strengths and weaknesses of global health preparedness. On the one hand, the swift identification of the virus, the rapid development of a vaccine, and the coordinated response of governments and health organizations were significant achievements. On the other hand, the challenges of communication, distribution, and public trust highlighted areas where improvements were needed.

The final death toll of the H1N1 pandemic was estimated to be between 151,700 and 575,400 people worldwide, with millions more infected. While this was far lower than the worst-case scenarios that had been feared, it was still a stark reminder of the potential dangers posed by novel influenza viruses.

The Legacy of H1N1: Lessons Learned and Moving Forward

The H1N1 pandemic of 2009-2010 was a wake-up call for the world, a reminder of the ever-present threat of influenza and the importance of vigilance, preparedness, and global cooperation. The experience of H1N1 led to several important lessons and changes in public health policy and practice. One of the most significant lessons was the need for better communication and public engagement during health crises. The mixed public reactions to H1N1 highlighted the importance of clear, accurate, and timely information, as well as the need to build and maintain public trust.

The pandemic also underscored the importance of investment in public health infrastructure and preparedness. Many countries took steps to improve their surveillance systems, stockpile essential medical supplies, and develop plans for future pandemics. The experience of H1N1 also led to greater collaboration among international organizations, governments, and the private sector, paving the way for more effective responses to future health threats.

The H1N1 pandemic also sparked renewed interest in influenza research, particularly in understanding the behavior of novel strains and developing more effective vaccines. The lessons learned from H1N1 would prove invaluable in the years to come, particularly during the COVID-19 pandemic, when the world once again faced a novel virus with the potential for global devastation.

Reflections on the H1N1 Pandemic

The H1N1 influenza pandemic of 2009-2010 was a complex and challenging event, one that tested the world's readiness to respond to a rapidly spreading virus. It was a pandemic marked by uncertainty, fear, and mixed reactions, but also by resilience, innovation, and progress. The story of H1N1 is a reminder of the unpredictable nature of pandemics and the need for constant vigilance, preparedness, and cooperation in the face of emerging health threats.

As we reflect on the H1N1 pandemic, we are reminded of the importance of science, communication, and global solidarity in protecting public health. The experience of H1N1 has left a lasting legacy, one that continues to shape the world's approach to infectious diseases and public health preparedness. It is a story of lessons learned, challenges overcome, and a reminder of the ever-present need to be ready for the next pandemic, whatever form it may take.

Part 13: The Ebola Outbreaks (1976, 2014-2016)

Ebola, a name that has become synonymous with fear and death, represents one of the most terrifying viral threats known to humankind. First identified in 1976, this highly lethal virus emerged from the dense, tropical forests of central Africa and quickly gained notoriety for its ability to cause severe hemorrhagic fever and high mortality rates. The world's understanding of Ebola evolved significantly over the years, but it was the outbreak of 2014-2016 that truly highlighted both the horrors of the disease and the global effort required to prevent a catastrophic pandemic. This chapter delves into the fear, suspense, and resilience that characterized these outbreaks, with a focus on the dramatic containment efforts, personal stories from the front lines, and the international response to avert a global crisis.

The First Encounter: 1976 in Zaire and Sudan

The Ebola virus first made its appearance in 1976 in two simultaneous outbreaks in Zaire (now the Democratic Republic of Congo) and Sudan. In a remote village near the Ebola River, a man named Mabalo Lokela became the first known victim of the virus. He arrived at the Yambuku Mission Hospital with a high fever, severe headache, muscle pain, and bloody diarrhea. The medical staff, unfamiliar with the new disease, treated him with the standard protocols for malaria and typhoid, common in the region. However, Lokela's condition worsened rapidly, and he succumbed to the illness within days.

The virus spread swiftly through Yambuku, primarily through the reuse of unsterilized needles at the mission hospital. The disease's progression was rapid and horrifying: high fever, vomiting, diarrhea, internal and external bleeding. Patients often died within a week, their bodies ravaged by the virus. Fear gripped the village and surrounding areas as more people fell ill and died. The local community, not understanding the nature of the outbreak, attributed it to witchcraft or malevolent spirits.

In Sudan, a similar outbreak occurred in Nzara, linked to a cotton factory where workers began showing symptoms of the same mysterious and deadly illness. Panic spread as more workers and their families fell ill. In both outbreaks, the mortality rate was shockingly high—around 88% in Zaire and 53% in Sudan.

The international community was quick to respond, sending teams of virologists and doctors to investigate. The virus was isolated, and it was given the name "Ebola," after the river near the outbreak in Zaire. Containment measures were implemented, including isolating the sick, tracing and monitoring contacts, and educating the public on how to prevent the spread of the virus. Within a few months, the outbreaks were brought under control, but the fear they inspired lingered. The world had witnessed the emergence of a new, deadly virus with no known cure or treatment.

Fear and Suspense: The Lethal Nature of Ebola

Ebola's lethality and the gruesome nature of its symptoms have made it one of the most feared viruses in the world. The virus attacks the body's blood vessels, causing them to leak and leading to severe internal and external bleeding. This hemorrhagic aspect, coupled with the rapid deterioration of the patient, contributes to the disease's terrifying reputation.

The fear surrounding Ebola is compounded by its mode of transmission. The virus spreads through direct contact with the blood, secretions, organs, or other bodily fluids of infected people, as well as through surfaces and materials contaminated with these fluids. In the context of limited healthcare infrastructure, especially in remote villages in Africa, this mode of transmission poses a significant challenge to containment efforts.

During the 1976 outbreaks, the lack of knowledge about the virus led to significant confusion and panic. People were afraid to go to hospitals, believing that they would become infected there. Some communities resorted to traditional healers, while others isolated themselves, hoping to avoid the disease. The fear was palpable, and the suspense of not knowing who might fall ill next added to the psychological toll of the outbreaks.

The 2014-2016 Outbreak: A Global Wake-Up Call

After the initial outbreaks in the 1970s, Ebola remained largely confined to sporadic, localized outbreaks in Africa. However, in 2014, the virus resurfaced with unprecedented force, triggering the largest and deadliest outbreak to date. The outbreak began in a small village in Guinea, West Africa, where a two-year-old boy known as Patient Zero fell ill and died. From there, the virus spread to neighboring Liberia and Sierra Leone, countries with porous borders, weak healthcare systems, and limited experience dealing with such a virulent pathogen.

Within months, the outbreak had spiraled out of control, spreading to urban centers and major cities. In Monrovia, the capital of Liberia, the situation was dire. Hospitals were overwhelmed, and many healthcare workers became infected, further straining an already stretched healthcare system. The streets of

Monrovia were filled with the sick and dying, and the fear of Ebola permeated every aspect of daily life.

The international community initially reacted slowly to the outbreak, underestimating the potential for widespread transmission. By the time the World Health Organization declared the Ebola outbreak a Public Health Emergency of International Concern in August 2014, the virus had already spread to multiple countries and claimed thousands of lives. The world was now facing a pandemic threat.

Dramatic Moments of Containment Efforts

The response to the 2014-2016 Ebola outbreak required a massive international effort, involving governments, non-governmental organizations (NGOs), and health agencies from around the world. The U.S. Centers for Disease Control and Prevention (CDC), the WHO, Médecins Sans Frontières (Doctors Without Borders), and other organizations deployed thousands of health workers to the affected regions. These frontline workers faced unimaginable challenges as they worked to contain the virus and treat the sick.

One of the most dramatic moments of the containment effort occurred in September 2014, when Liberian authorities, in an attempt to curb the spread of the virus, quarantined the densely populated West Point neighborhood in Monrovia. The quarantine, enforced by armed soldiers, sparked panic and unrest among residents, who were cut off from the rest of the city and feared they would be left to die. Tensions escalated, and clashes between residents and security forces erupted. The quarantine, though controversial, highlighted the extreme measures that were being considered to contain the virus's spread.

In Sierra Leone, health workers faced similar challenges. Entire villages were placed under quarantine, with food and medical supplies delivered by helicopter. Makeshift treatment centers were set up in tents and abandoned buildings, where doctors and nurses, clad in protective suits, worked tirelessly to care for the sick. The extreme heat, the constant risk of infection, and the sheer scale of the outbreak made their work both physically and emotionally exhausting.

In Guinea, local and international health workers faced additional challenges related to cultural practices, such as traditional burial rites that involved washing and touching the bodies of the deceased. These practices, while culturally significant, facilitated the transmission of the virus. Efforts to educate communities on safer burial practices were met with resistance and suspicion, complicating containment efforts.

Personal Stories from the Front Lines

Amidst the fear and chaos, countless stories of courage, sacrifice, and resilience emerged. One of the most poignant stories is that of Dr. Sheik Humarr Khan, a leading Sierra Leonean doctor specializing in viral hemorrhagic fevers. Dr. Khan, who had been at the forefront of the fight against Ebola, contracted the virus in July 2014 while treating patients at the Kenema Government Hospital. Despite the best efforts of his colleagues, Dr. Khan succumbed to the virus, becoming one of the many healthcare workers who lost their lives in the battle against Ebola.

In Liberia, a nurse named Salome Karwah became an international symbol of resilience after surviving Ebola. Karwah, who contracted the virus while caring for her father, brother, and pregnant mother—all of whom died from Ebola—survived against all odds. After recovering, she returned to the Ebola treatment center where she had been a patient, this time as a healthcare worker. Karwah's story of survival and determination provided hope and inspiration to many during the darkest days of the outbreak.

The international volunteers who flocked to West Africa also brought with them stories of bravery and compassion. Healthcare workers from around the world, including doctors, nurses, and public health specialists, risked their lives to help contain the outbreak. Many contracted the virus themselves, and some, like Dr. Ian Crozier, an infectious disease specialist from the United States, became gravely ill. Dr. Crozier was evacuated to the United States and treated in a specialized isolation unit, where he eventually recovered. His battle with Ebola was harrowing and underscored the personal risks faced by those on the front lines.

The International Response: Preventing a Global Catastrophe

The international response to the 2014-2016 Ebola outbreak was unprecedented in scale and scope. The United States, the European Union, China, and other countries provided financial assistance, medical supplies, and personnel to support the containment efforts. The United Nations established the United Nations Mission for Ebola Emergency Response (UNMEER), the first-ever UN emergency health mission, to coordinate the international response and ensure a swift and effective effort to contain the virus.

Airports around the world implemented health screenings for passengers arriving from affected regions, and airlines suspended flights to West Africa. In the United States, the CDC established an emergency operations center and worked closely with state and local health departments to monitor travelers, provide guidance, and prepare for the possibility of imported cases.

Despite these efforts, the international response faced numerous challenges. The scale of the outbreak, coupled with the limited healthcare infrastructure in the affected countries, made containment efforts difficult. In some cases, international assistance was slow to arrive, and coordination between various organizations was hampered by bureaucratic hurdles and logistical difficulties.

Containment and Relief: The Outbreak's End

By early 2015, the situation began to improve. The coordinated international response, combined with the heroic efforts of local and international health workers, started to pay off. New cases began to decline, and the outbreak, which had seemed unstoppable just months earlier, was gradually brought under control. By June 2016, the WHO declared the end of the Ebola outbreak in West Africa, marking the conclusion of the deadliest Ebola epidemic in history.

The relief felt across the affected countries was immense, but so too was the recognition of the profound human and economic toll of the outbreak. The epidemic had claimed over 11,000 lives and infected more than 28,000 people. Entire communities were devastated, and the long-term social and economic impacts were severe. In the wake of the outbreak, efforts were made to rebuild and strengthen healthcare systems, improve surveillance and response capacities, and ensure that the lessons learned from Ebola would not be forgotten.

The Legacy of Ebola: Preparedness and Vigilance

The Ebola outbreaks of 1976 and 2014-2016 left an indelible mark on global public health. They highlighted the importance of rapid response, international cooperation, and community engagement in managing infectious disease outbreaks. The 2014-2016 outbreak, in particular, underscored the need for global preparedness and the capacity to respond swiftly to emerging health threats.

In the aftermath of the outbreak, significant efforts were made to improve global health security. The WHO implemented reforms to strengthen its ability to respond to health emergencies, and the Global Health Security Agenda (GHSA) was launched to enhance global capacities to prevent, detect, and respond to infectious disease threats. The development of the rVSV-ZEBOV vaccine, which showed high efficacy in preventing Ebola infection, was a major breakthrough and provided a new tool for combating future outbreaks.

The Ebola outbreak also underscored the importance of addressing the social and cultural dimensions of public health. The success of containment efforts often depended on the ability to engage communities, build trust, and respect cultural practices while promoting safe behaviors. These lessons continue to inform public health strategies in managing other infectious diseases and health crises.

Reflections on the Ebola Outbreaks

The Ebola outbreaks of 1976 and 2014-2016 were harrowing reminders of the unpredictable and deadly nature of infectious diseases. They revealed both the vulnerabilities and the strengths of human societies in the face of such threats. The fear and suspense that accompanied these outbreaks were matched by the resilience, courage, and determination of those who fought to contain the virus and save lives.

As we reflect on the Ebola outbreaks, we are reminded of the importance of preparedness, vigilance, and international cooperation in safeguarding global health. The stories of those who lived through these outbreaks—of those who fought on the front lines, those who survived against all odds, and those who lost their lives—serve as a testament to the human spirit's capacity to endure and overcome even the most formidable challenges. The legacy of Ebola is not just one of fear and death, but also of hope, resilience, and the enduring commitment to prevent future outbreaks and protect the health of all people.

Part 14: The COVID-19 Pandemic (2019-Present)

In late 2019, the world was brimming with optimism, preparing to enter a new decade with hopes of peace, prosperity, and progress. However, in the shadow of this optimism, an unseen enemy was silently taking root. In the bustling city of Wuhan, China, a novel coronavirus, later named SARS-CoV-2, began to spread, marking the beginning of what would become the COVID-19 pandemic. This global health crisis would bring unprecedented social and economic upheaval, testing the resilience of societies worldwide, and sparking a race against time for a vaccine. The pandemic's story is one of fear, confusion, and uncertainty, but also of remarkable resilience, adaptation, and the relentless pursuit of scientific innovation.

The First Cases: An Unknown Virus Emerges

In December 2019, doctors in Wuhan, a major transportation hub in central China, began noticing a series of unusual pneumonia cases among patients with ties to the Huanan Seafood Wholesale Market. The patients exhibited symptoms of a respiratory infection: fever, cough, and shortness of breath. However, unlike other respiratory illnesses, this new disease seemed to spread rapidly and unpredictably, with some patients developing severe respiratory distress that required intensive care.

Local health authorities initially suspected a new strain of pneumonia and began investigating. Samples from the patients were collected and sent to laboratories for analysis. On December 31, 2019, Chinese health officials reported the cluster of pneumonia cases to the World Health Organization (WHO), alerting the international community to a potential new public health threat.

Within days, the virus was identified as a novel coronavirus, closely related to the coronaviruses responsible for the SARS (Severe Acute Respiratory Syndrome) outbreak in 2003 and MERS (Middle East Respiratory Syndrome) in 2012. This new virus, later named SARS-CoV-2, had an alarming ability to spread between humans, sparking concern among global health experts.

Despite efforts to contain the virus in Wuhan, the disease—now known as COVID-19 (Coronavirus Disease 2019)—continued to spread.

The Sudden Global Spread: A Pandemic Unfolds

By January 2020, the virus had spread beyond China's borders, carried by international travelers to countries across Asia, Europe, and North America. Cases began appearing in Thailand, Japan, South Korea, and eventually the United States. The virus spread like wildfire, and it became clear that this was not a localized outbreak but a rapidly escalating global pandemic.

The speed of the virus's spread was unprecedented. In a matter of weeks, COVID-19 had reached every continent except Antarctica. Countries like Italy and Iran became new epicenters of the outbreak, with hospitals overwhelmed and death tolls climbing daily. In February 2020, northern Italy faced a crisis as its healthcare system teetered on the brink of collapse. Hospitals in Lombardy were filled to capacity, and medical staff, exhausted and under-equipped, struggled to keep up with the influx of critically ill patients.

In March 2020, the WHO officially declared COVID-19 a pandemic. Governments around the world scrambled to respond, implementing emergency measures to slow the virus's spread. Borders were closed, flights were canceled, and cities locked down. For many, the reality of the pandemic set in with a sense of disbelief and fear. Streets emptied, businesses shuttered, and a palpable sense of unease settled over the world.

Fear and Confusion in the Early Days

The early days of the pandemic were marked by confusion and fear. With little known about the virus, misinformation spread rapidly, fueling panic and uncertainty. Social media and news outlets were flooded with conflicting reports, conspiracy theories, and sensationalized headlines, making it difficult for people to discern fact from fiction. Some downplayed the severity of the virus, while others warned of an impending catastrophe.

In the absence of clear information, fear took hold. Supermarkets were besieged by panic buyers stockpiling essentials like toilet paper, canned goods, and hand sanitizer. In cities around the world, shelves were stripped bare, reflecting the anxiety and uncertainty gripping the public. Hospitals braced for an influx of patients, and healthcare workers, lacking adequate protective equipment, faced the terrifying prospect of becoming infected themselves.

The fear was not just about the virus itself but also about the unknown. How did it spread? How deadly was it? Who was most at risk? Without clear answers, people turned to drastic measures to protect themselves. Masks, once a rare sight outside of healthcare settings in many countries, became a symbol of the pandemic, worn by millions as a protective barrier against an invisible threat.

The Race Against Time: Developing a Vaccine

As the virus spread, scientists and researchers around the world launched an unprecedented effort to develop a vaccine. The race for a vaccine became a global priority, seen as the only way to bring the pandemic under control and return life to normal. Traditionally, vaccine development takes years, if not decades, but the urgency of the pandemic compressed this timeline dramatically.

Pharmaceutical companies, academic institutions, and governments poured resources into vaccine research, collaborating and competing in a race against time. The development of a COVID-19 vaccine became a high-stakes endeavor, driven by a sense of urgency and the potential for enormous financial and humanitarian rewards.

The challenge was immense. The virus was new, and there was no prior immunity in the population. Additionally, the technology to rapidly develop a vaccine was still in its infancy. However, advances in biotechnology, particularly mRNA technology, offered a promising path forward. Companies like Moderna and Pfizer-BioNTech quickly adapted their mRNA platforms to target the spike protein of SARS-CoV-2, the part of the virus that allows it to enter human cells.

By July 2020, several vaccine candidates had entered clinical trials, a remarkable feat given the timeline. The world watched with bated breath as researchers conducted phase after phase of trials, testing the vaccines' safety and efficacy. The suspense was palpable, with every update scrutinized by a public desperate for a solution. In November 2020, the first promising results were announced: Pfizer-BioNTech's mRNA vaccine demonstrated over 90% efficacy in preventing COVID-19. Soon after, Moderna's vaccine showed similarly encouraging results.

Challenges of Lockdowns and Public Health Measures

While the race for a vaccine offered hope, the world had to confront the immediate challenges of containing the virus. Governments implemented a range of public health measures to curb transmission, including lockdowns, social distancing, mask mandates, and travel restrictions. These measures, though necessary, came with significant social and economic costs.

Lockdowns became a defining feature of the pandemic. In countries like Italy, Spain, and later the United States and the United Kingdom, strict stay-at-home orders were enforced, with only essential services allowed to operate. Streets that were once bustling with activity fell silent. In some cities, military and police patrolled the streets to enforce compliance. The psychological impact of these lockdowns was profound. Isolation, anxiety, and uncertainty became commonplace as people struggled to cope with the new reality.

The economic impact was equally severe. Businesses closed, jobs were lost, and entire industries were upended. The hospitality, travel, and retail sectors were hit particularly hard, with many companies forced into bankruptcy. Governments scrambled to provide economic relief, introducing stimulus packages, unemployment benefits, and business loans to keep economies afloat. Yet, despite these efforts, the economic fallout was immense, with millions worldwide pushed into poverty and economic insecurity.

Schools were closed, forcing students to shift to online learning. This transition highlighted stark inequalities, as not all students had access to the necessary technology or a conducive environment for remote education. Parents, now juggling work from home and their children's education, faced unprecedented stress.

Resilience and Adaptation: Societies Respond to the Crisis

Despite the immense challenges, societies around the world demonstrated remarkable resilience and adaptability. Communities rallied together, finding innovative ways to support one another. In Italy, residents sang from their balconies, creating a sense of solidarity and hope in the face of despair. In cities worldwide, volunteer networks sprang up to deliver food and medicine to the elderly and vulnerable.

The pandemic also accelerated technological adoption and innovation. Remote work, once a niche practice, became the norm for millions of workers. Companies rapidly adapted to new realities, adopting digital tools and platforms to facilitate communication and collaboration. Telehealth emerged as a critical service, allowing patients to consult doctors without risking exposure to the virus.

The scientific community, too, showed extraordinary adaptability. Researchers pivoted quickly to study the virus, its transmission, and potential treatments. New collaborations were formed, data was shared openly, and traditional barriers to research and development were broken down in the name of urgent progress. The speed and scale of scientific response to COVID-19 were unprecedented, reflecting both the urgency of the crisis and the potential of global collaboration.

Personal Stories: Courage and Sacrifice on the Front Lines

Amidst the global upheaval, countless personal stories of courage, sacrifice, and resilience emerged. Healthcare workers were on the front lines of the battle against COVID-19, risking their lives to save others. In hospitals from New York to London to Mumbai, doctors, nurses, and support staff worked tirelessly, often without adequate protective equipment, to care for an ever-growing number of patients. Many contracted the virus themselves, and some lost their lives.

In Wuhan, the initial epicenter of the outbreak, Dr. Li Wenliang, an ophthalmologist who first raised the alarm about the virus, became a symbol of the sacrifices made by healthcare workers. After warning his colleagues about the virus in late December 2019, Dr. Li was reprimanded by local authorities for "spreading rumors." He later contracted COVID-19 and died in February 2020, sparking an outpouring of grief and anger. His death underscored the risks faced by those on the front lines and highlighted the importance of transparency and openness in managing health crises.

In the United States, Nurse Kious Kelly, working in a New York City hospital overwhelmed with COVID-19 patients, became one of the first healthcare workers in the U.S. to die from the virus. His death highlighted the severe lack of personal protective equipment (PPE) in hospitals and the extraordinary risks faced by medical staff. Stories like those of Dr. Li and Nurse Kelly served as powerful reminders of the human cost of the pandemic and the courage of those who fought it.

Vaccination Rollout and the Road to Recovery

With the emergency authorization of the first COVID-19 vaccines in December 2020, the world entered a new phase of the pandemic: the mass vaccination campaign. Countries launched massive logistical efforts to distribute and administer vaccines, starting with healthcare workers, the elderly, and those most at risk. The rollout was met with both hope and challenges.

Some countries, particularly wealthy nations, secured large quantities of vaccines early on, allowing them to vaccinate significant portions of their populations quickly. In other parts of the world, however, vaccine access was limited, exacerbating global inequalities. Efforts by initiatives like COVAX aimed to provide equitable access to vaccines, but challenges persisted in distribution and production.

The vaccine rollout was not without controversy. In some regions, vaccine hesitancy emerged as a significant barrier, fueled by misinformation, distrust of government, and concerns about the speed of vaccine development. Public health campaigns focused on educating the public and building trust, but the challenges were considerable.

Despite these hurdles, the vaccination campaigns made significant progress. By mid-2021, millions of people worldwide had been vaccinated, providing a path toward reopening and recovery. Schools and businesses began to reopen, and travel slowly resumed. However, the emergence of new variants of the virus, including the Delta and Omicron variants, posed ongoing challenges, reminding the world that the fight against COVID-19 was far from over.

The Massive Social and Economic Impacts

The social and economic impacts of the COVID-19 pandemic were vast and far-reaching. The global economy contracted sharply in 2020, with the worst downturn since the Great Depression. Millions of people lost their jobs, and entire sectors, such as tourism and hospitality, were devastated. Small businesses, in particular, struggled to survive amidst prolonged lockdowns and reduced consumer spending.

The pandemic also exacerbated existing inequalities. The impact was disproportionately felt by low-income workers, women, and minority communities. Many of these groups were more likely to be employed in sectors that could not transition to remote work, such as retail, hospitality, and frontline services. Additionally, the shift to online education and remote work highlighted disparities in access to technology and the internet, further widening the gap between the privileged and the disadvantaged.

Mental health became a significant concern, as prolonged isolation, fear, and economic uncertainty took a toll on people's well-being. Reports of anxiety, depression, and other mental health issues surged, prompting calls for greater mental health support and services.

Despite these challenges, the pandemic also catalyzed positive social changes. Communities came together to support one another, volunteering their time and resources to help those in need. Businesses and governments demonstrated remarkable adaptability, finding new ways to operate and deliver services. The pandemic also prompted a reevaluation of work-life balance, with many workers demanding greater flexibility and a focus on well-being.

Resilience and Adaptation: Societies Moving Forward

As the world slowly emerged from the grips of the pandemic, the resilience and adaptability of societies became evident. The experience of COVID-19 led to profound changes in how we live, work, and interact. Remote work, once a rarity, became a permanent fixture in many sectors, with companies adopting hybrid models that allowed employees to work both in-office and remotely.

The pandemic also accelerated technological innovation. The use of digital tools and platforms soared, transforming education, healthcare, commerce, and entertainment. Telehealth became a mainstream service, providing patients with access to medical care from the safety of their homes. E-commerce thrived as consumers turned to online shopping, prompting retailers to expand their digital presence and capabilities.

The scientific community continued to adapt and innovate. Researchers around the world studied the virus and its variants, developed new treatments, and monitored the long-term effects of COVID-19. The rapid development of vaccines demonstrated the potential of mRNA technology, opening new possibilities for vaccine development against other diseases.

Reflections on the COVID-19 Pandemic

The COVID-19 pandemic has been a defining event of the 21st century, a global crisis that tested the resilience of individuals, communities, and nations. It was a pandemic marked by fear, confusion, and uncertainty, but also by remarkable resilience, adaptability, and the relentless pursuit of scientific progress. The pandemic exposed vulnerabilities in global health systems, highlighted the importance of preparedness and collaboration, and underscored the need for equity and solidarity in responding to global challenges.

As we reflect on the COVID-19 pandemic, we are reminded of the fragility of life and the interconnectedness of our world. The stories of those who fought on the front lines, the sacrifices made by healthcare workers, and the resilience of communities provide a testament to the strength of the human spirit. The lessons learned from this pandemic will continue to shape our approach to public health, preparedness, and global cooperation in the years to come.

The COVID-19 pandemic is not just a story of loss and suffering, but also one of hope, resilience, and the enduring human capacity to adapt and overcome. It has challenged us to think differently, act swiftly, and work together in the face of unprecedented challenges. As the world continues to navigate the ongoing impacts of the pandemic, these lessons will be crucial in building a more resilient, equitable, and prepared global community.

Part 15: Pandemics and Globalization

The 21st century is often described as the age of globalization—a period marked by unprecedented interconnectedness in trade, travel, and communication. While globalization has brought immense benefits, such as economic growth, cultural exchange, and technological advancement, it has also facilitated the rapid spread of infectious diseases. The relationship between pandemics and globalization is complex and multifaceted, characterized by both the vulnerabilities and the strengths that interconnectedness brings. From the Black Death in the 14th century to the COVID-19 pandemic in the 21st, pandemics have exposed the delicate balance between the benefits of a connected world and the risks it poses. This chapter explores this dynamic, building suspense around how globalization has shaped both the spread of diseases and the global response, using case studies of past pandemics to illustrate this relationship.

The Dual-Edged Sword of Globalization

Globalization, defined as the process by which the world becomes increasingly interconnected through the movement of goods, people, and ideas, has been a defining characteristic of human civilization. It has accelerated in recent centuries due to advances in technology, transportation, and communication. While globalization has brought many positive outcomes, it has also created new pathways for the spread of infectious diseases. In a globalized world, a virus can travel across continents in a matter of hours, turning a local outbreak into a global pandemic almost overnight.

The Black Death of the 14th century is one of the earliest examples of how globalization can facilitate the spread of disease. The plague, caused by the bacterium *Yersinia pestis*, is believed to have originated in Central Asia and spread westward along the Silk Road, a network of trade routes that connected the East and West. As merchants and travelers moved goods and people across vast distances, they unwittingly carried the plague with them. The disease eventually reached Europe, where it decimated the population, killing an estimated 25 million people—about one-third of the continent's population.

The spread of the Black Death was not only a consequence of trade but also of increased urbanization. As people flocked to cities in search of economic opportunities, they lived in crowded conditions with poor sanitation, creating ideal conditions for the spread of infectious diseases. The interconnectedness that facilitated trade and economic growth also made it easier for the plague to spread rapidly from one city to another, demonstrating the dual-edged sword of globalization.

Case Study: The Spread of the Spanish Flu (1918-1919)

The Spanish Flu pandemic of 1918-1919 is another example of how globalization can amplify the spread of infectious diseases. The pandemic emerged in the final months of World War I, a time when millions of soldiers and civilians were on the move across Europe and beyond. The war had created a global network of troop movements, supply chains, and refugee flows, which provided the perfect conditions for the rapid spread of the virus.

The Spanish Flu is believed to have originated in a military camp in the United States before spreading to Europe with American troops. Once in Europe, the virus spread quickly among the troops and then to civilian populations, aided by the dense, unsanitary conditions of the trenches and the crowded cities. The global nature of the war meant that the virus could easily hitch a ride on ships and trains, spreading from Europe to Asia, Africa, and the Americas. In less than a year, the Spanish Flu had infected about one-third of the world's population and claimed an estimated 50 million lives.

The pandemic revealed the vulnerabilities of a globalized world. The same networks that facilitated the movement of people and goods also allowed the virus to spread rapidly across borders, demonstrating how interconnectedness can transform a local outbreak into a global health crisis. At the same time, the response to the Spanish Flu also highlighted the limitations of global cooperation. Many countries, still recovering from the devastation of World War I, were slow to coordinate their responses, and there was little international collaboration in the early stages of the pandemic.

Globalization and the HIV/AIDS Epidemic

The HIV/AIDS epidemic, which emerged in the late 20th century, further illustrates the complex relationship between pandemics and globalization. HIV, the virus that causes AIDS, is believed to have crossed over from chimpanzees to humans in Central Africa in the early 20th century. For decades, the virus circulated at low levels in isolated communities. However, by the 1970s and 1980s, as globalization accelerated, HIV began to spread more widely.

Several factors contributed to the global spread of HIV. Increased air travel allowed the virus to cross continents, while urbanization and economic migration brought people into closer contact in cities, where the virus could spread more easily. The global sex trade, driven by economic disparities and facilitated by improved transportation, also played a role in the spread of HIV. Additionally, the use of contaminated blood products and intravenous drug use further facilitated the transmission of the virus across different regions.

The global response to HIV/AIDS was initially slow, hindered by stigma, misinformation, and lack of coordination. However, as the scale of the epidemic became apparent, a more coordinated international response emerged. Organizations like UNAIDS, along with initiatives like the Global Fund to Fight AIDS, Tuberculosis, and Malaria, brought together governments, NGOs, and the private sector to address the epidemic. The global response to HIV/AIDS demonstrated how interconnectedness could also facilitate cooperation and shared learning, providing a model for managing future pandemics.

The 21st Century: SARS, H1N1, and the Globalization of Health Risks

The 21st century has seen several pandemics that underscore the relationship between globalization and infectious diseases. The SARS outbreak of 2002-2003 was a wake-up call for the world. The virus, a novel coronavirus, emerged in southern China and quickly spread to Hong Kong, a major international hub. From there, it spread to over 20 countries, carried by international travelers. The SARS outbreak demonstrated how a virus could spread rapidly in a globalized world, moving from one continent to another in a matter of days.

The response to SARS also highlighted the potential for globalization to facilitate a coordinated international response. The World Health Organization (WHO) played a critical role in coordinating the global response, issuing travel advisories, providing guidance to affected countries, and facilitating information sharing. The lessons learned from SARS led to significant improvements in global health surveillance and response systems, which would prove invaluable in managing future outbreaks.

The H1N1 influenza pandemic of 2009-2010 provided another example of how globalization can amplify the spread of infectious diseases. The virus, a novel strain of influenza, emerged in Mexico and quickly spread to over 200 countries, aided by international air travel and global trade networks. The rapid spread of H1N1 underscored the vulnerabilities of a globalized world, where a virus could quickly move from one country to another. However, it also demonstrated the potential for a coordinated global response, with the WHO, national governments, and international organizations working together to develop and distribute vaccines, provide guidance, and monitor the spread of the virus.

Case Study: The COVID-19 Pandemic (2019-Present)

The COVID-19 pandemic is perhaps the most compelling example of the relationship between pandemics and globalization. The virus, SARS-CoV-2, emerged in Wuhan, China, a major transportation hub, in late 2019. Within weeks, it had spread to multiple countries, aided by international travel and trade networks. By March 2020, COVID-19 had been declared a pandemic by the WHO, and countries around the world were grappling with the unprecedented challenge of managing a rapidly spreading virus in a highly interconnected world.

COVID-19 spread with alarming speed, moving from one country to another via international travelers. The virus's ability to spread asymptomatically made containment even more challenging, as individuals who appeared healthy could unknowingly spread the virus to others. The global nature of trade and travel meant that no country was immune, and the virus quickly reached every corner of the globe.

The pandemic exposed the vulnerabilities of globalization. The same networks that facilitate global trade and travel also allowed the virus to spread rapidly across borders. However, the pandemic also demonstrated the potential for a coordinated global response. The rapid development and distribution of COVID-19 vaccines were made possible by unprecedented international collaboration and cooperation. Scientists, governments, and private companies around the world worked together to develop, test, and distribute vaccines in record time, demonstrating the potential for globalization to facilitate a collective response to global health threats.

Global Health Governance and the Role of International Organizations

The relationship between pandemics and globalization has also highlighted the importance of global health governance and the role of international organizations in managing health crises. The World Health Organization (WHO) has played a central role in coordinating the global response to pandemics, providing guidance, facilitating information sharing, and supporting countries in their efforts to contain outbreaks.

The experience of recent pandemics has underscored the need for a strong and effective global health governance framework. The International Health Regulations (IHR), revised in 2005 in response to the SARS outbreak, provide a framework for international cooperation in managing health emergencies. The IHR require countries to report certain disease outbreaks and public health events to the WHO and provide a mechanism for coordinated international response.

However, the COVID-19 pandemic has also exposed some of the limitations of the current global health governance framework. The initial response to COVID-19 was marked by delays, lack of coordination, and inadequate preparedness in many countries. The pandemic highlighted the need for stronger international cooperation, greater investment in public health infrastructure, and more robust mechanisms for sharing information and resources.

The Future of Pandemics and Globalization

As the world continues to become more interconnected, the relationship between pandemics and globalization will remain a critical issue for global health. The experience of past pandemics has demonstrated both the vulnerabilities and the strengths of a globalized world. On the one hand, globalization has facilitated the rapid spread of infectious diseases, turning local outbreaks into global crises almost overnight. On the other hand, globalization has also facilitated a coordinated international response, enabling countries to share information, resources, and expertise in managing health threats.

Looking ahead, the challenge will be to harness the benefits of globalization while mitigating its risks. This will require a continued focus on strengthening global health systems, improving surveillance and response capacities, and fostering international cooperation and solidarity. It will also require a commitment to addressing the social, economic, and environmental factors that contribute to the emergence and spread of infectious diseases, including climate change, deforestation, and economic inequality.

The COVID-19 pandemic has provided a stark reminder of the potential for pandemics to disrupt societies and economies on a global scale. It has also demonstrated the importance of preparedness, resilience, and adaptation in managing such crises. As the world moves forward, the lessons learned from COVID-19 and other pandemics will be crucial in shaping a more resilient and prepared global community, capable of responding to the challenges of a globalized world.

Reflections on Pandemics and Globalization

The relationship between pandemics and globalization is complex and multifaceted, characterized by both the vulnerabilities and the strengths that interconnectedness brings. The history of pandemics, from the Black Death to COVID-19, illustrates how globalization has facilitated the spread of infectious diseases while also enabling a coordinated international response. The dual-edged sword of globalization presents both challenges and opportunities for global health.

As we reflect on this relationship, we are reminded of the need for vigilance, preparedness, and cooperation in managing the risks associated with a globalized world. The lessons learned from past pandemics provide a roadmap for future efforts to prevent and respond to infectious disease outbreaks. By building stronger, more resilient health systems, fostering international collaboration, and addressing the root causes of emerging health threats, we can better protect the health and well-being of people everywhere.

The story of pandemics and globalization is not just one of risk and vulnerability, but also one of resilience, adaptation, and the power of collective action. It is a story that continues to evolve, as the world navigates the complex and interconnected landscape of the 21st century. The future will undoubtedly bring new challenges, but with the lessons of the past as our guide, we can face them with confidence, solidarity, and a commitment to protecting global health.

Part 16: Social and Cultural Transformations in the Wake of Pandemics

Throughout history, pandemics have been catalysts for profound social and cultural transformations. These global health crises have forced societies to confront their vulnerabilities, rethink their values, and adapt to new realities. The impact of pandemics extends far beyond the immediate loss of life and economic disruption; they leave lasting imprints on the social fabric, reshaping cultural norms, behaviors, and institutions. From the Black Death in the 14th century to the COVID-19 pandemic in the 21st century, the story of pandemics is also a story of social upheaval and cultural adaptation, marked by moments of intense fear, resilience, and profound change.

The Black Death: A Turning Point in European Society

The Black Death, which swept through Europe in the mid-14th century, was one of the deadliest pandemics in history, killing an estimated 25 million people—about one-third of Europe's population. The sheer scale of the mortality created an atmosphere of fear and uncertainty, leading to significant social and cultural transformations. As the plague spread, it brought with it not just death, but also profound changes in the way people lived, worked, and viewed the world around them.

The sudden and massive loss of life caused by the Black Death led to a dramatic shift in social structures. With a significant portion of the population dead, labor became scarce, and the value of labor increased. This shift in the balance of power between landowners and laborers had profound economic and social implications. Peasants, who had long been tied to the land under feudal obligations, found themselves in a position to demand higher wages and better working conditions. In some regions, the scarcity of labor even led to the collapse of the feudal system altogether, paving the way for the rise of a more market-based economy.

Culturally, the Black Death also prompted a reevaluation of religious and spiritual beliefs. As the plague ravaged cities and villages, people turned to the

Church for answers, seeking solace and understanding in their faith. However, the Church's inability to explain or stop the plague led to a crisis of faith for many. The authority of the Church was called into question, and new religious movements emerged, some advocating for greater piety and penance, while others challenged the Church's teachings and practices. This period of religious upheaval set the stage for the Protestant Reformation in the 16th century.

The cultural impact of the Black Death was also evident in the arts and literature of the time. The pervasive sense of death and despair found expression in works like Giovanni Boccaccio's *The Decameron*, a collection of stories told by a group of young people sheltering from the plague in a villa outside Florence. The theme of death became a central motif in European art, with macabre imagery such as the *Danse Macabre* (Dance of Death) reflecting the collective trauma and existential uncertainty brought about by the pandemic.

The Spanish Flu and the Roaring Twenties

The Spanish Flu pandemic of 1918-1919, which coincided with the end of World War I, caused widespread social and cultural upheaval. The flu, which killed an estimated 50 million people worldwide, struck at a time when the world was already reeling from the devastation of war. The pandemic compounded the trauma of the war, creating a sense of disillusionment and despair that permeated much of society.

In the immediate aftermath of the Spanish Flu, there was a pervasive sense of anxiety and uncertainty. The war had already shattered many of the old social and cultural norms, and the flu further exacerbated this process. Traditional social structures and hierarchies were challenged as people grappled with the massive loss of life and the existential threat posed by the pandemic. This period of upheaval paved the way for significant social and cultural changes in the 1920s.

The decade following the pandemic, known as the Roaring Twenties, was characterized by a cultural explosion and a break from traditional norms. There was a sense of urgency and hedonism, as people sought to live life to the fullest in the wake of the pandemic and war. Jazz music, flapper fashion, and new forms of entertainment like cinema and radio became symbols of a new, modern era. Women's roles in society began to change as well, with more women entering the workforce and challenging traditional gender norms.

At the same time, the Spanish Flu prompted new approaches to public health and medicine. The pandemic underscored the importance of hygiene, sanitation, and vaccination, leading to greater investment in public health infrastructure and research. Governments around the world began to take a more active role in managing public health, recognizing the need for coordinated responses to prevent future pandemics.

HIV/AIDS and the Transformation of LGBTQ+ Rights

The HIV/AIDS epidemic, which emerged in the 1980s, had a profound impact on social and cultural norms, particularly around issues of sexuality, stigma, and rights. The epidemic initially affected gay men disproportionately, leading to widespread fear, discrimination, and stigma. Many LGBTQ+ individuals faced intense social ostracism and were blamed for the spread of the disease. The initial response to the epidemic was marked by fear, prejudice, and a lack of urgency from governments and health organizations.

However, the HIV/AIDS epidemic also galvanized a powerful social and cultural movement that transformed attitudes toward LGBTQ+ rights and health. Activists within the LGBTQ+ community organized to demand attention, resources, and research for those affected by the disease. Groups like ACT UP (AIDS Coalition to Unleash Power) and the Gay Men's Health Crisis (GMHC) emerged as powerful voices advocating for change, using direct action and civil disobedience to challenge government inaction and societal prejudice.

The HIV/AIDS epidemic also fostered greater visibility and acceptance of LGBTQ+ individuals. As the epidemic spread, it became clear that HIV/AIDS was not confined to any one group, and that stigma and discrimination only hindered efforts to combat the disease. This realization helped to shift public perceptions, leading to greater empathy and support for LGBTQ+ rights. The activism and advocacy that emerged in response to HIV/AIDS played a critical role in advancing LGBTQ+ rights, culminating in significant legal and social changes in the decades that followed.

Culturally, the HIV/AIDS epidemic had a profound impact on the arts and media. Artists, writers, and filmmakers used their platforms to raise awareness about the epidemic and challenge stereotypes and stigma. Works like Tony Kushner's *Angels in America* and the musical *Rent* brought the realities of HIV/AIDS to a wider audience, fostering greater understanding and empathy. The epidemic also inspired a new wave of community-based art and activism, as people used creative expression to process their grief, anger, and hope.

The SARS Outbreak and the Rise of Digital Connectivity

The SARS outbreak of 2002-2003, while relatively contained in terms of its geographic spread and mortality, had a significant social and cultural impact, particularly in Asia. The outbreak, caused by a novel coronavirus, led to widespread fear and uncertainty, particularly in countries like China, Hong Kong, and Singapore. The rapid spread of SARS and the dramatic public health measures implemented to contain it—such as quarantines, travel restrictions, and school closures—had a lasting impact on societal behaviors and attitudes.

One of the most significant social transformations brought about by SARS was the rise of digital connectivity and communication. During the outbreak, many people turned to digital platforms to stay connected, share information, and access services. Schools and universities quickly adopted online learning, businesses moved to remote work, and social gatherings shifted to digital spaces. This early experience with digital connectivity set the stage for the rapid digital transformation that would occur in the following decades, particularly in response to the COVID-19 pandemic.

The SARS outbreak also led to a greater emphasis on public health and hygiene in many Asian societies. The use of face masks, which became commonplace during the SARS outbreak, continued to be a common sight in many parts of Asia, particularly during flu seasons or pollution events. The outbreak heightened awareness of the importance of public health measures, leading to stronger surveillance systems, better preparedness, and more robust responses to future outbreaks.

Case Study: COVID-19 and the Social Fabric of the 21st Century

The COVID-19 pandemic, which began in late 2019 and continues to affect the world, has been a defining event of the 21st century, causing profound social and cultural transformations. The pandemic has upended daily life, altering how people work, learn, socialize, and interact with one another. It has exposed vulnerabilities and inequalities in societies, reshaped cultural norms, and prompted new ways of thinking about community, resilience, and well-being.

One of the most visible social transformations brought about by COVID-19 has been the shift to remote work and digital communication. With lockdowns and social distancing measures in place, millions of people worldwide transitioned to working from home, leading to a reimagining of the traditional workplace. Companies adopted digital tools and platforms to facilitate remote collaboration, and many organizations have since embraced hybrid work models as a permanent feature. This shift has had significant implications for work-life balance, productivity, and the future of work.

The pandemic also accelerated the adoption of digital technologies in education, healthcare, and commerce. Schools and universities moved to online learning, prompting a rapid digital transformation in the education sector. Telehealth emerged as a critical service, allowing patients to access medical care from the safety of their homes. E-commerce and contactless payment systems became more prevalent as consumers turned to online shopping and digital transactions to minimize physical contact.

COVID-19 also prompted a reevaluation of social norms and behaviors. The widespread adoption of mask-wearing, social distancing, and hand hygiene reflected a new awareness of public health and safety. In many countries, the pandemic prompted discussions about the importance of community, solidarity, and collective responsibility. Mutual aid networks and volunteer initiatives sprang up to support vulnerable populations, reflecting a renewed emphasis on community care and social solidarity.

However, the pandemic also exposed and exacerbated existing social inequalities. Low-income workers, women, and minority communities were disproportionately affected by the economic and health impacts of the pandemic. The digital divide became more apparent as remote work and online learning highlighted disparities in access to technology and the internet. These inequalities sparked discussions about social justice, equity, and the need for systemic change.

Cultural Adaptations and the Arts in Times of Pandemic

Pandemics have always influenced cultural production, and COVID-19 has been no exception. Artists, writers, and filmmakers have responded to the pandemic in various ways, using their work to process the collective trauma, explore themes of isolation and connection, and envision new futures. Virtual concerts, online theater performances, and digital art exhibitions became new ways of engaging with the arts, highlighting the resilience and adaptability of cultural institutions.

The pandemic also inspired new forms of creative expression, as people turned to art, music, and writing to cope with the challenges of lockdown and isolation. Social media platforms became spaces for sharing art, stories, and experiences, fostering a sense of global community and solidarity. Memes, videos, and digital content reflecting pandemic experiences became a new form of cultural expression, capturing the humor, frustration, and hope of a world in crisis.

The cultural adaptations brought about by COVID-19 reflect a broader trend of resilience and creativity in the face of adversity. The arts have always played a critical role in helping societies navigate crises, providing a space for reflection, healing, and imagining new possibilities. As the world continues to grapple with the ongoing impacts of the pandemic, the role of culture in fostering resilience and adaptation remains as important as ever.

Reflections on Social and Cultural Transformations in the Wake of Pandemics

Pandemics have been powerful catalysts for social and cultural change throughout history. They have forced societies to confront their vulnerabilities, adapt to new realities, and rethink their values and priorities. From the economic and social upheaval of the Black Death to the digital transformations accelerated by COVID-19, pandemics have reshaped the social fabric in profound ways.

As we reflect on these transformations, we are reminded of the resilience and adaptability of human societies in the face of crisis. The story of pandemics is not just one of fear and loss, but also one of innovation, solidarity, and cultural renewal. It is a story that continues to evolve, shaped by the ongoing interplay between disease, society, and culture.

The social and cultural transformations brought about by pandemics also highlight the importance of collective action, empathy, and creativity in navigating crises. They remind us that while pandemics can bring significant challenges, they also offer opportunities for reflection, growth, and change. As the world moves forward, the lessons learned from past pandemics will be crucial in shaping a more resilient, equitable, and culturally rich future.

Part 17: Economic Disruptions and Recovery Efforts

Pandemics have historically been catalysts for economic disruption, causing sudden downturns that ripple across industries, markets, and nations. From the collapse of trade routes during the Black Death to the shuttering of businesses during the COVID-19 pandemic, the economic impact of pandemics has been profound and far-reaching. However, in the wake of these crises, societies have also demonstrated remarkable resilience and innovation, finding new ways to rebuild and recover. This chapter explores the economic disruptions caused by pandemics, the suspenseful uncertainty that accompanies economic downturns, and the stories of resilience and innovation that have emerged in their aftermath.

Economic Disruptions of the Black Death: A New Order Emerges

The Black Death, which swept through Europe in the mid-14th century, was not only a demographic catastrophe but also a profound economic disruption. The pandemic decimated the population, killing an estimated one-third of Europe's inhabitants. This massive loss of life had immediate and far-reaching economic consequences, disrupting agricultural production, collapsing trade routes, and causing widespread labor shortages.

The sudden and dramatic reduction in the population led to a sharp decline in demand for goods and services. Markets shrank, and many businesses, particularly those reliant on trade and transport, went bankrupt. The suspension of trade routes, as cities and ports were quarantined to prevent the spread of the plague, further exacerbated the economic downturn. As merchants and travelers were unable to move freely, the once-thriving trade networks that connected Europe to Asia and Africa ground to a halt.

The labor shortages caused by the Black Death were perhaps the most significant economic disruption. With so many workers dead, the supply of labor plummeted, leading to a sharp rise in wages. Surviving workers found themselves in a position to demand better pay and conditions, leading to a series of labor uprisings and revolts across Europe. In England, the Peasants' Revolt of 1381 was a direct result of the social and economic upheaval caused by the Black Death, as peasants demanded an end to serfdom and greater rights.

The economic disruptions caused by the Black Death also led to significant structural changes in the economy. With fewer workers available, there was a shift away from labor-intensive agriculture toward more efficient forms of production. Landowners, faced with the high cost of labor, began to experiment with new agricultural techniques and crops, laying the groundwork for the agricultural innovations of the Renaissance. The decline of the feudal system and the rise of a more market-oriented economy were also direct consequences of the economic turmoil caused by the plague.

The Spanish Flu and the Economic Aftermath of World War I

The Spanish Flu pandemic of 1918-1919 occurred in the immediate aftermath of World War I, a time of significant economic uncertainty and upheaval. The war had already caused immense economic disruption, with massive military expenditures, destruction of infrastructure, and loss of life. The Spanish Flu, which killed an estimated 50 million people worldwide, further compounded these economic challenges.

The pandemic disrupted labor markets, as millions of workers fell ill or died. In some industries, particularly those requiring physical labor or close contact, such as manufacturing and transportation, the workforce was severely depleted. This disruption led to reduced productivity and increased costs, as companies struggled to maintain operations with a diminished workforce. In some regions, particularly in the United States and Europe, the flu caused temporary closures of factories, mines, and other critical infrastructure, leading to further economic losses.

The economic impact of the Spanish Flu was also felt in global trade. With shipping and transport networks already weakened by the war, the pandemic caused additional disruptions. Many ports and borders were closed to prevent the spread of the virus, leading to delays and shortages of goods. The global economy, already fragile from the war, faced new challenges as countries grappled with the dual shocks of the flu and the economic downturn.

Despite these challenges, the post-pandemic period also saw remarkable economic resilience and innovation. In the United States, the 1920s were characterized by a period of rapid economic growth and technological advancement. Known as the "Roaring Twenties," this era saw the rise of new industries, such as automobiles, aviation, and consumer electronics, as well as significant improvements in productivity and living standards. The economic recovery was driven in part by pent-up demand and the desire to rebuild after years of war and pandemic, as well as by technological innovations that transformed industries and markets.

HIV/AIDS and the Economic Impact on Developing Countries

The HIV/AIDS epidemic, which emerged in the 1980s and continues to affect millions worldwide, has had profound economic implications, particularly in developing countries. Unlike other pandemics, HIV/AIDS is a long-term, chronic disease that affects individuals over many years, leading to a sustained economic impact.

In many developing countries, particularly in sub-Saharan Africa, HIV/AIDS has had a devastating impact on the labor force. The disease disproportionately affects young adults, who are often the most economically productive members of society. As a result, HIV/AIDS has led to a significant loss of labor, reducing economic output and productivity. In some countries, the epidemic has wiped out entire generations of workers, leaving behind a weakened workforce and a significant strain on social services and healthcare systems.

The economic impact of HIV/AIDS extends beyond the loss of labor. The epidemic has also increased healthcare costs, as governments and households struggle to provide treatment and care for those affected. In some countries, the cost of antiretroviral drugs, hospital care, and support services has placed a significant burden on already strained public health systems. The epidemic has also disrupted education, as children orphaned by HIV/AIDS are forced to leave school to care for younger siblings or work to support their families.

Despite these challenges, the response to HIV/AIDS has also spurred economic innovation and resilience. Many countries have developed innovative public health strategies to manage the epidemic, including community-based care models, public-private partnerships, and social enterprises. The global response to HIV/AIDS, including initiatives like the Global Fund to Fight AIDS, Tuberculosis, and Malaria, has also provided significant funding and resources to affected countries, helping to strengthen healthcare systems and improve economic resilience.

The SARS Outbreak and Economic Vulnerabilities

The SARS outbreak of 2002-2003, while relatively contained geographically, had significant economic repercussions, particularly in Asia. The outbreak, caused by a novel coronavirus, led to widespread fear and uncertainty, causing consumers to stay home and businesses to close temporarily. The economic impact was felt most acutely in sectors reliant on travel and tourism, such as airlines, hotels, and retail.

The SARS outbreak exposed vulnerabilities in the global economy, particularly in the context of rapidly growing interconnectedness and interdependence. In Hong Kong, the economy contracted sharply as tourist arrivals plummeted and consumer spending declined. The real estate market, already vulnerable to economic fluctuations, was also affected, with property prices falling as economic activity slowed.

The economic disruptions caused by SARS prompted governments and businesses to rethink their approaches to risk management and resilience. In Singapore, for example, the government introduced a range of economic measures to support businesses and workers affected by the outbreak, including wage subsidies, tax relief, and loan guarantees. These measures helped to cushion the economic impact and laid the groundwork for a more resilient economy.

The outbreak also highlighted the importance of diversification and adaptability in the face of economic shocks. Many businesses in affected regions began to diversify their supply chains, develop contingency plans, and invest in digital technologies to mitigate future risks. These efforts to build resilience would prove invaluable in managing the economic challenges posed by future pandemics, including COVID-19.

Case Study: The Economic Fallout of the COVID-19 Pandemic

The COVID-19 pandemic, which began in late 2019 and continues to affect the world, has caused unprecedented economic disruption on a global scale. The pandemic has upended economies, disrupted global trade, and led to the most significant economic downturn since the Great Depression. The economic impact of COVID-19 has been profound and multifaceted, affecting every sector and region of the world.

The initial economic shock of COVID-19 was caused by widespread lockdowns and social distancing measures implemented to slow the spread of the virus. Businesses closed, supply chains were disrupted, and consumer spending plummeted. The travel and tourism sectors were among the hardest hit, with airlines grounding fleets, hotels closing, and international travel coming to a standstill. In the United States alone, unemployment rates soared to levels not seen since the Great Depression, with millions of workers losing their jobs or being furloughed.

The economic uncertainty caused by COVID-19 also led to significant volatility in financial markets. Stock markets around the world experienced sharp declines in the early months of the pandemic, reflecting investor concerns about the economic impact of the virus and the potential for a prolonged recession. Central banks and governments responded with unprecedented fiscal and monetary stimulus measures, including interest rate cuts, quantitative easing, and massive economic relief packages.

The economic impact of COVID-19 has been uneven, with some sectors and regions hit harder than others. While the pandemic has been devastating for industries reliant on physical interaction, such as hospitality, retail, and entertainment, it has also accelerated growth in sectors such as e-commerce, digital services, and healthcare. Companies that were able to adapt quickly to the new reality, leveraging digital technologies and flexible business models, have shown remarkable resilience.

Stories of Resilience and Innovation in the Wake of COVID-19

Despite the immense economic challenges posed by COVID-19, the pandemic has also been a catalyst for resilience and innovation. Businesses, governments, and individuals have demonstrated remarkable adaptability in finding new ways to operate, connect, and thrive in the face of unprecedented disruption.

One notable story of resilience comes from the manufacturing sector. As supply chains were disrupted and demand for certain products surged, manufacturers quickly adapted their operations to meet new needs. Companies that traditionally produced automotive parts or electronics, for example, retooled their factories to produce ventilators, personal protective equipment (PPE), and other critical medical supplies. This rapid pivot not only helped to address shortages but also demonstrated the potential for agile and adaptable manufacturing processes.

The pandemic has also spurred innovation in the digital economy. With millions of people working from home and relying on digital platforms for communication, shopping, and entertainment, technology companies have seen unprecedented growth. Companies like Zoom, Amazon, and Netflix experienced a surge in demand, prompting rapid innovation and scaling efforts. The shift to remote work has also accelerated the adoption of digital tools and platforms, from cloud computing to collaborative software, transforming how businesses operate and interact with customers.

In the realm of healthcare, COVID-19 has prompted significant innovation in both public health and medical research. The rapid development and deployment of COVID-19 vaccines, achieved in record time, represents a remarkable achievement in scientific innovation and collaboration. Additionally, the pandemic has spurred advancements in telehealth, remote monitoring, and data analytics, transforming how healthcare is delivered and managed.

At the community level, the pandemic has also inspired grassroots resilience and innovation. In cities around the world, mutual aid networks and community organizations have mobilized to provide support to those most affected by the pandemic, from delivering groceries and medicines to organizing virtual events and support groups. These efforts have demonstrated the power of community and solidarity in times of crisis, providing a blueprint for future resilience and recovery efforts.

Economic Recovery Efforts: Building Back Better

As the world emerges from the COVID-19 pandemic, attention has turned to economic recovery and the question of how to build back better. The pandemic has exposed deep vulnerabilities and inequalities in the global economy, prompting calls for a more inclusive, sustainable, and resilient recovery.

Governments around the world have launched ambitious recovery plans, investing in infrastructure, green energy, and digital transformation to stimulate growth and create jobs. The European Union's €750 billion recovery fund, for example, is aimed at supporting member states in their recovery efforts, with a focus on green and digital transitions. In the United States, the Biden administration's American Rescue Plan includes significant investments in infrastructure, healthcare, and education, as well as direct support for individuals and businesses affected by the pandemic.

The recovery from COVID-19 also presents an opportunity to address long-standing social and economic inequalities. The pandemic has highlighted the need for stronger social safety nets, better healthcare systems, and more equitable access to opportunities. As countries rebuild, there is a growing recognition of the importance of investing in human capital, from education and skills development to mental health and social services, to create a more inclusive and resilient economy.

Reflections on Economic Disruptions and Recovery Efforts

The economic disruptions caused by pandemics are often sudden, severe, and far-reaching, creating an atmosphere of uncertainty and fear. Yet, as history has shown, these crises also provide opportunities for resilience, innovation, and transformation. The story of economic disruptions and recovery efforts is one of adaptation, creativity, and the enduring human spirit to overcome adversity.

As we reflect on the economic impacts of past pandemics, we are reminded of the importance of preparedness, adaptability, and solidarity in navigating economic shocks. The resilience and innovation demonstrated in the wake of these crises provide valuable lessons for the future, highlighting the potential for recovery and renewal even in the face of the most daunting challenges.

The economic disruptions caused by pandemics are not just stories of loss and hardship but also of hope, resilience, and the power of human ingenuity. As the world continues to recover from COVID-19 and prepare for future challenges, these stories serve as a testament to the strength of the global community and the potential for building a more resilient, equitable, and sustainable economy.

Part 18: The Evolution of Public Health Responses

Pandemics have been a recurring challenge throughout human history, each time testing the resilience and ingenuity of societies worldwide. As each new pandemic unfolds, it brings with it lessons and opportunities for growth, driving the evolution of public health responses. The story of public health is one of constant adaptation, marked by suspenseful developments of new strategies and technologies, successes and failures, and a continual quest to better understand and combat infectious diseases. This chapter explores the evolution of public health responses to pandemics, focusing on the dramatic changes in approaches and the development of technologies over time.

The Early Days: Isolation and Quarantine

The concept of quarantine is one of the earliest forms of public health response to infectious disease, dating back to the medieval period. The term "quarantine" originates from the Italian word *quaranta giorni*, meaning "forty days," referring to the 40-day isolation period imposed on ships arriving in Venice during the Black Death in the 14th century. As the plague ravaged Europe, killing millions, cities like Venice adopted the practice of quarantining incoming ships, cargo, and passengers to prevent the spread of the disease.

Quarantine and isolation became fundamental strategies in the public health response to infectious diseases, particularly during times of plague. In many European cities, specialized quarantine facilities, known as *lazarettos*, were established to house travelers and goods suspected of carrying the plague. These facilities were often located on islands or in remote areas, where infected individuals could be isolated from the general population.

While quarantine was an effective strategy in reducing the spread of disease, it was not without its challenges and limitations. The implementation of quarantine measures was often inconsistent, and the lack of understanding of the nature of infectious diseases meant that quarantine was sometimes applied too late or incorrectly. Furthermore, quarantine measures could have severe economic and social consequences, disrupting trade and causing hardship for those subjected to isolation.

Despite these limitations, quarantine and isolation remained the primary tools in the public health arsenal for centuries. The practice of quarantine was formalized in the 18th and 19th centuries, with many countries establishing quarantine laws and regulations to control the spread of infectious diseases, particularly cholera, which emerged as a significant public health threat in the 19th century.

The Germ Theory Revolution: A New Understanding of Disease

The 19th century marked a turning point in the understanding and management of infectious diseases, driven by the development of the germ theory of disease. The germ theory, which posited that microorganisms such as bacteria and viruses were the causative agents of infectious diseases, revolutionized public health and laid the groundwork for modern microbiology and epidemiology.

The germ theory of disease was first proposed in the mid-19th century by scientists such as Louis Pasteur and Robert Koch. Pasteur's experiments with fermentation and the spoilage of food led him to conclude that microorganisms were responsible for both processes, while Koch's work with anthrax and tuberculosis provided clear evidence that specific bacteria caused specific diseases.

The acceptance of the germ theory had profound implications for public health responses to pandemics. It led to the development of new strategies and technologies to prevent and control infectious diseases, including sanitation, vaccination, and antimicrobial treatments. The germ theory also provided a scientific basis for understanding how diseases spread, leading to the development of epidemiology as a discipline.

One of the most significant public health successes of the germ theory era was the development of vaccines. The concept of vaccination had been around since Edward Jenner's discovery of the smallpox vaccine in the late 18th century, but it was the germ theory that provided the scientific foundation for the development of vaccines for other diseases. In the late 19th and early 20th centuries, vaccines were developed for several deadly diseases, including cholera, plague, typhoid, and tuberculosis.

The Sanitary Movement and Public Health Infrastructure

The germ theory of disease also gave rise to the sanitary movement, a public health reform movement that emerged in the 19th century in response to the unsanitary living conditions in rapidly growing cities. The sanitary movement advocated for improved public health infrastructure, including clean water supply, sewage disposal, and waste management, as essential measures to prevent the spread of infectious diseases.

The cholera pandemics of the 19th century played a critical role in shaping the sanitary movement and the development of public health infrastructure. Cholera, a highly infectious disease caused by the bacterium *Vibrio cholerae*, spread rapidly through contaminated water and food, causing severe diarrhea and dehydration. The repeated outbreaks of cholera in Europe and North America highlighted the need for better sanitation and public health measures.

One of the most significant achievements of the sanitary movement was the development of modern water and sewage systems. In London, the construction of the London sewer system in the mid-19th century, designed by engineer Joseph Bazalgette, was a direct response to the cholera outbreaks and the Great Stink of 1858, when the River Thames was overwhelmed with untreated sewage. The new sewer system helped to reduce the incidence of waterborne diseases and laid the foundation for modern urban sanitation.

The sanitary movement also led to the establishment of public health institutions and regulatory frameworks. In the United Kingdom, the Public Health Act of 1848 marked the beginning of state intervention in public health, establishing local boards of health and appointing medical officers to oversee sanitation and disease prevention efforts. Similar developments occurred in other countries, with public health departments and agencies being established to manage infectious disease outbreaks and promote public health.

20th Century Advances: Vaccination and Antibiotics

The 20th century saw significant advances in public health responses to pandemics, driven by developments in medical science and technology. Two of the most important breakthroughs were the development of vaccines and the discovery of antibiotics, which transformed the ability to prevent and treat infectious diseases.

Vaccination became a cornerstone of public health strategy in the 20th century, with the development of vaccines for a wide range of infectious diseases. The success of vaccination campaigns in eradicating smallpox, one of the deadliest diseases in human history, stands as one of the greatest achievements in public health. The smallpox vaccine, first developed by Edward Jenner in the late 18th century and later improved by subsequent researchers, became widely available in the 20th century, leading to the global eradication of the disease by 1980.

The discovery of antibiotics in the 20th century revolutionized the treatment of bacterial infections. The first antibiotic, penicillin, was discovered by Alexander Fleming in 1928, and its mass production during World War II marked a turning point in the fight against infectious diseases. Antibiotics provided an effective means of treating bacterial infections that had previously been untreatable, significantly reducing mortality rates and transforming medical practice.

However, the reliance on antibiotics also led to new challenges, particularly the emergence of antibiotic-resistant bacteria. The overuse and misuse of antibiotics in both human medicine and agriculture have contributed to the development of antibiotic-resistant strains, posing a significant threat to global public health. The rise of antibiotic resistance underscores the need for ongoing research and innovation in the development of new treatments and public health strategies.

Case Study: The Global Response to HIV/AIDS

The emergence of HIV/AIDS in the 1980s presented a new challenge for public health, requiring a coordinated global response and innovative approaches to disease management and prevention. Unlike many other infectious diseases, HIV/AIDS is a chronic condition that requires long-term management and care, presenting unique challenges for public health systems.

The initial public health response to HIV/AIDS was hampered by stigma, discrimination, and a lack of understanding of the disease. Early efforts to control the epidemic focused on behavior change, with public health campaigns promoting safe sex practices, needle exchange programs, and blood screening to reduce transmission. These strategies, while effective in certain contexts, were often limited by social and cultural barriers, as well as a lack of access to healthcare services.

The global response to HIV/AIDS also highlighted the importance of community-based approaches and the involvement of affected populations in public health strategies. Activist groups, such as ACT UP and the Treatment Action Campaign, played a critical role in advocating for greater access to treatment and care, challenging stigma and discrimination, and promoting awareness and education about HIV/AIDS. These efforts helped to shift the public health response from a top-down approach to a more community-centered model.

The development of antiretroviral therapy (ART) in the mid-1990s marked a turning point in the fight against HIV/AIDS. ART provided an effective means of managing the disease, reducing viral load, and preventing transmission. The introduction of ART transformed HIV/AIDS from a death sentence to a manageable chronic condition, significantly reducing mortality rates and improving the quality of life for millions of people living with HIV.

However, the global response to HIV/AIDS also faced significant challenges, particularly in terms of access to treatment and care. In many low- and middle-income countries, the high cost of antiretroviral drugs and limited healthcare infrastructure posed significant barriers to access. The establishment of initiatives like the Global Fund to Fight AIDS, Tuberculosis, and Malaria and the U.S. President's Emergency Plan for AIDS Relief (PEPFAR) helped to address these challenges by providing funding, resources, and support to affected countries.

21st Century Innovations: Digital Health and Genomic Surveillance

The 21st century has brought new challenges and opportunities for public health responses to pandemics, driven by advances in digital health, genomic surveillance, and data analytics. These innovations have transformed the ability to detect, monitor, and respond to infectious disease outbreaks in real time, providing new tools for public health professionals and policymakers.

Digital health technologies, including mobile health applications, telemedicine, and electronic health records, have played a critical role in modern public health responses. During the COVID-19 pandemic, digital health tools were widely used to monitor the spread of the virus, track contacts, and provide remote care and support to patients. Mobile health applications, such as contact tracing apps, helped to identify and isolate cases quickly, reducing transmission and supporting public health efforts.

Genomic surveillance, which involves the sequencing and analysis of viral genomes, has emerged as a powerful tool in the fight against pandemics. The rapid sequencing of the SARS-CoV-2 genome in early 2020 provided critical insights into the origins and spread of the virus, enabling the development of diagnostic tests and guiding public health interventions. Genomic surveillance has also been used to track the emergence of new variants, informing vaccine development and public health strategies.

Data analytics and modeling have become increasingly important in public health responses to pandemics, providing valuable insights into the spread and impact of infectious diseases. Advanced modeling techniques, such as agent-based modeling and machine learning, have been used to predict the course of outbreaks, assess the impact of interventions, and optimize resource allocation. These tools have enabled more effective and targeted public health responses, improving the ability to manage and contain pandemics.

Successes and Failures: Lessons from Past Pandemics

The evolution of public health responses to pandemics is a story of both successes and failures, reflecting the complexity and challenges of managing infectious disease outbreaks. While there have been significant advances in public health strategies and technologies, there have also been notable failures and missed opportunities.

One of the key successes in the history of public health is the global eradication of smallpox, achieved through a coordinated vaccination campaign led by the World Health Organization (WHO). The eradication of smallpox demonstrated the power of vaccination and international cooperation in combating infectious diseases, providing a model for future public health efforts.

However, there have also been significant failures in public health responses to pandemics. The initial response to the HIV/AIDS epidemic was marked by stigma, discrimination, and a lack of urgency, contributing to the rapid spread of the virus and high mortality rates. Similarly, the response to the COVID-19 pandemic was hampered by delays, lack of coordination, and inadequate preparedness in many countries, highlighting the need for stronger global health governance and more effective public health systems.

The failures of past public health responses underscore the importance of learning from history and continually improving strategies and approaches. The experience of pandemics has highlighted the need for greater investment in public health infrastructure, stronger surveillance and response systems, and more equitable access to healthcare and resources. It has also emphasized the importance of community engagement, communication, and trust-building in managing infectious disease outbreaks.

The Future of Public Health: Preparing for the Next Pandemic

As the world continues to grapple with the ongoing impacts of the COVID-19 pandemic, there is a growing recognition of the need to strengthen public health systems and prepare for future pandemics. The experience of past pandemics has provided valuable lessons and insights that can inform future public health efforts.

One of the key priorities for future public health preparedness is the development of more robust surveillance and response systems. This includes investing in early warning systems, improving data collection and sharing, and enhancing genomic surveillance capabilities. The ability to detect and respond to outbreaks quickly is critical to preventing the spread of infectious diseases and minimizing their impact.

Another priority is the development of new vaccines, treatments, and diagnostic tools. The rapid development of COVID-19 vaccines demonstrated the potential of new technologies, such as mRNA, to accelerate vaccine development. Continued investment in research and innovation is essential to developing effective countermeasures for emerging infectious diseases and addressing the challenge of antimicrobial resistance.

Finally, there is a need to strengthen global health governance and cooperation. The COVID-19 pandemic has highlighted the importance of international collaboration in managing pandemics, from sharing information and resources to coordinating responses and supporting affected countries.

Strengthening global health governance frameworks, such as the International Health Regulations (IHR), and promoting greater equity and solidarity in global health efforts will be critical to building a more resilient and prepared world.

Reflections on the Evolution of Public Health Responses

The evolution of public health responses to pandemics is a story of adaptation, innovation, and resilience. From the early days of quarantine and isolation to the development of vaccines and digital health technologies, public health has continually evolved to meet the challenges posed by infectious diseases. The successes and failures of past pandemics provide valuable lessons for the future, highlighting the importance of preparedness, collaboration, and innovation in safeguarding global health.

As we reflect on the evolution of public health responses, we are reminded of the enduring human capacity to learn, adapt, and overcome in the face of adversity. The story of public health is not just one of science and medicine but also one of community, solidarity, and the collective effort to protect and promote the health and well-being of all people.

The future of public health will undoubtedly bring new challenges and opportunities, but with the lessons of the past as our guide, we can face them with confidence, resilience, and a commitment to building a healthier and more equitable world for all.

Part 19: The Future of Pandemics and Global Health Security

As the world navigates the aftermath of the COVID-19 pandemic, the question of what lies ahead in terms of global health security and future pandemics looms large. The 21st century has already witnessed several significant outbreaks—from SARS to Ebola to COVID-19—each exposing vulnerabilities in global health systems and highlighting the need for greater preparedness. The future of pandemics is marked by uncertainty, with emerging threats on the horizon and ongoing efforts to bolster global defenses against infectious diseases. This chapter explores the future of pandemics, building suspense around potential threats and the challenges of preparing for them, while examining the ethical and practical considerations in global health security.

Emerging Threats: The Next Pandemic

The world today is more interconnected than ever before, and this interconnectedness brings both opportunities and risks. One of the most significant risks is the potential for new and emerging infectious diseases to spread rapidly across borders, turning local outbreaks into global pandemics. The future of pandemics is likely to be shaped by several key factors, including climate change, urbanization, globalization, and the ongoing evolution of pathogens.

Climate change is expected to play a significant role in shaping the landscape of future pandemics. Rising temperatures, changing precipitation patterns, and shifting ecosystems are likely to alter the distribution of vectors such as mosquitoes and ticks, which transmit diseases like malaria, dengue, and Lyme disease. Warmer climates may expand the range of these vectors, exposing new populations to diseases previously confined to specific regions. Additionally, melting permafrost and ice may release ancient pathogens, potentially reintroducing diseases that have been dormant for thousands of years.

Urbanization is another factor contributing to the risk of future pandemics. As more people move into cities, the population density increases, creating ideal conditions for the rapid spread of infectious diseases. Urban areas often have high levels of mobility and interconnectedness, with people traveling frequently and interacting in crowded spaces. This can facilitate the transmission of pathogens, turning cities into hotspots for outbreaks. The COVID-19 pandemic demonstrated how quickly a virus could spread in densely populated urban centers, overwhelming healthcare systems and causing significant social and economic disruption.

The ongoing evolution of pathogens also poses a threat to global health security. Pathogens, particularly viruses, are constantly mutating, adapting to new environments and hosts. This evolutionary process can lead to the emergence of new strains that are more transmissible, virulent, or resistant to existing treatments. The emergence of antibiotic-resistant bacteria, driven by the overuse and misuse of antibiotics, is a growing concern, with the potential to render existing treatments ineffective and create a new wave of drug-resistant infections.

The Role of Surveillance and Early Detection

One of the critical elements in preparing for future pandemics is the development and enhancement of surveillance and early detection systems. Early detection of an outbreak is essential for preventing its spread and mitigating its impact. Effective surveillance systems can help identify unusual patterns of illness, track the spread of disease, and provide early warnings to public health authorities.

Advances in digital health technologies, genomic sequencing, and data analytics have transformed the landscape of disease surveillance, providing new tools for detecting and monitoring infectious diseases. Digital health platforms, including mobile health applications and electronic health records, enable real-time data collection and analysis, facilitating early detection and response. Genomic sequencing allows for the rapid identification of pathogens and their variants, providing critical information for guiding public health interventions and developing vaccines and treatments.

Despite these advancements, there are still significant challenges to effective surveillance and early detection. One of the main challenges is the lack of global standardization and coordination in surveillance systems. Many countries have limited resources and infrastructure for surveillance, resulting in gaps in data collection and reporting. Additionally, political and social factors can hinder timely reporting and response, as seen in the initial stages of the COVID-19 pandemic. Building a more robust and coordinated global surveillance system will be essential for improving early detection and response to future pandemics.

Preparing for the Unknown: Scenario Planning and Simulation Exercises

Given the uncertainty surrounding future pandemics, scenario planning and simulation exercises have become critical tools for preparedness. These exercises allow public health authorities, governments, and organizations to test their response plans, identify gaps and weaknesses, and develop strategies for managing different types of outbreaks.

Scenario planning involves developing and analyzing different hypothetical scenarios to anticipate potential challenges and responses. These scenarios can range from localized outbreaks of known diseases to global pandemics caused by novel pathogens. By considering various scenarios, organizations can better understand the potential risks and develop contingency plans to address them.

Simulation exercises, or "tabletop exercises," are a more hands-on approach to preparedness, allowing participants to practice their response to a simulated outbreak. These exercises often involve multiple stakeholders, including public health agencies, emergency services, hospitals, and government officials, and are designed to test coordination, communication, and decision-making in a crisis. The lessons learned from these exercises can inform future planning and improve overall readiness for a pandemic.

One notable example of a simulation exercise is Event 201, held in October 2019 by the Johns Hopkins Center for Health Security in partnership with the World Economic Forum and the Bill & Melinda Gates Foundation. Event 201 simulated a global pandemic caused by a novel coronavirus, highlighting the challenges of managing a rapidly spreading virus in a highly interconnected world. The exercise underscored the importance of global coordination, communication, and public-private collaboration in responding to pandemics.

Innovations in Vaccine Development and Distribution

The rapid development and deployment of COVID-19 vaccines have been hailed as a remarkable scientific achievement, demonstrating the potential for new technologies to accelerate vaccine development. The success of mRNA vaccines, developed by Pfizer-BioNTech and Moderna, has opened new possibilities for vaccine development, providing a platform that can be adapted quickly to target new pathogens.

Looking ahead, the focus on vaccine innovation will likely continue, with efforts to develop "universal" vaccines that can provide protection against a broad range of pathogens. Researchers are also exploring new delivery methods, such as needle-free vaccines and oral vaccines, to improve accessibility and uptake, particularly in low-resource settings.

The COVID-19 pandemic has also highlighted the importance of equitable vaccine distribution. The stark disparities in vaccine access between high-income and low-income countries have underscored the need for a more equitable global health system. Initiatives like COVAX, the global vaccine-sharing program, have aimed to address these disparities, but challenges remain in ensuring timely and equitable access to vaccines for all populations.

Building a more resilient global health system will require addressing the barriers to vaccine access, including intellectual property rights, production capacity, and distribution logistics. Strengthening local production capabilities, investing in infrastructure, and promoting technology transfer will be essential for improving vaccine access and equity in future pandemics.

The Role of Global Health Security Governance

The COVID-19 pandemic has underscored the importance of global health security governance and the need for stronger international cooperation in managing pandemics. The World Health Organization (WHO) has played a central role in coordinating the global response to COVID-19, providing guidance, facilitating information sharing, and supporting countries in their efforts to contain the virus. However, the pandemic has also exposed limitations in the current global health governance framework, highlighting the need for reforms and improvements.

One of the key challenges in global health security governance is the lack of a binding international legal framework for pandemic preparedness and response. While the International Health Regulations (IHR), revised in 2005, provide a framework for managing public health emergencies, they lack enforcement mechanisms and rely on voluntary compliance by member states. Strengthening the IHR and developing a more robust legal framework for global health security will be critical for improving pandemic preparedness and response.

Another challenge is the need for greater investment in global health infrastructure and capacity-building. Many low- and middle-income countries lack the resources and infrastructure to manage infectious disease outbreaks effectively. Increasing funding for global health initiatives, such as the Global Fund to Fight AIDS, Tuberculosis, and Malaria, and supporting capacity-building efforts in vulnerable regions will be essential for improving global health security.

The role of international organizations, including the WHO, the World Bank, and the United Nations, will also be critical in coordinating and supporting global health security efforts. Strengthening these organizations, promoting greater collaboration, and ensuring adequate funding and resources will be essential for building a more resilient global health system.

Ethical Considerations in Pandemic Preparedness and Response

The future of pandemics and global health security also raises important ethical considerations. One of the key ethical challenges is the issue of equity and access to healthcare and resources. The COVID-19 pandemic has highlighted stark disparities in access to vaccines, treatments, and healthcare services, with marginalized and vulnerable populations often bearing the brunt of the impact. Ensuring equitable access to healthcare and resources will be critical for addressing the ethical dimensions of pandemic preparedness and response.

Another ethical consideration is the balance between individual rights and public health. Public health measures, such as lockdowns, quarantine, and contact tracing, often involve trade-offs between protecting public health and respecting individual freedoms and privacy. Navigating these ethical dilemmas will require careful consideration of the principles of proportionality, necessity, and fairness, as well as transparent communication and engagement with affected communities.

The use of digital technologies in pandemic response also raises ethical questions related to privacy, data security, and surveillance. Contact tracing apps, digital health platforms, and genomic surveillance technologies have been critical tools in managing the COVID-19 pandemic, but they also raise concerns about the potential for misuse and abuse of personal data. Developing ethical guidelines and frameworks for the use of digital technologies in public health will be essential for protecting individual rights and ensuring public trust.

Building Resilience: Community Engagement and Trust

Building resilience to future pandemics will require more than just technological innovation and international cooperation; it will also require strong community engagement and trust-building. The COVID-19 pandemic has highlighted the importance of engaging communities in public health efforts, from promoting vaccine uptake to encouraging adherence to public health measures.

Effective community engagement involves understanding and addressing the needs, concerns, and priorities of different populations. This includes working with community leaders, organizations, and stakeholders to develop culturally appropriate and context-specific public health strategies. Engaging communities in the planning and implementation of public health measures can help build trust, improve compliance, and enhance the effectiveness of interventions.

Trust is a critical component of public health responses to pandemics. Trust in public health authorities, healthcare systems, and vaccines is essential for ensuring the success of public health measures. Building and maintaining trust requires transparent communication, honesty, and accountability. Public health authorities must be proactive in addressing misinformation, providing clear and accurate information, and engaging with communities in meaningful ways.

The Role of Innovation and Research in Pandemic Preparedness

Innovation and research will continue to play a central role in pandemic preparedness and response. The rapid development of COVID-19 vaccines was a testament to the power of scientific innovation and collaboration. However, there is still much to learn and discover in the field of infectious diseases and public health.

Future research efforts should focus on understanding the underlying mechanisms of disease transmission, the role of host-pathogen interactions, and the factors that drive the emergence and spread of new pathogens. Research should also explore new technologies and approaches for preventing, diagnosing, and treating infectious diseases, including the development of novel vaccines, therapeutics, and diagnostics.

Collaboration and knowledge-sharing will be essential for advancing research and innovation in pandemic preparedness. Public-private partnerships, international collaborations, and interdisciplinary research efforts will be critical for driving progress and developing new solutions to the challenges posed by infectious diseases.

Reflections on the Future of Pandemics and Global Health Security

The future of pandemics is uncertain, but one thing is clear: the threat of infectious diseases will continue to challenge global health security. The lessons learned from past pandemics, including COVID-19, provide valuable insights into the complexities of managing pandemics and the importance of preparedness, innovation, and cooperation.

As we look to the future, there is a need for greater investment in global health infrastructure, stronger surveillance and response systems, and more equitable access to healthcare and resources. Building a more resilient global health system will require a commitment to ethical principles, community engagement, and trust-building, as well as a focus on innovation and research.

The future of pandemics and global health security is not just a story of emerging threats and challenges, but also a story of resilience, adaptation, and hope. By learning from the past, investing in the present, and preparing for the future, we can build a safer, healthier, and more equitable world for all.

Conclusion

Pandemics have been a recurring and transformative force throughout human history. From the Plague of Athens to the COVID-19 pandemic, each outbreak has left an indelible mark on societies, economies, and cultures. They have tested our resilience, exposed our vulnerabilities, and spurred advancements in medicine, public health, and technology. As we conclude this exploration of pandemics, it is essential to recap the key themes and insights that have emerged, reflect on human resilience and adaptation, and consider the lessons learned from our historical encounters with these formidable adversaries.

Recap of Key Themes and Insights

The narrative of pandemics is one of cyclical challenge and response, where human societies have continuously been forced to confront the perils of infectious diseases. Several key themes have emerged throughout this exploration:

- **Interconnectedness and Vulnerability:** One of the most significant insights from studying pandemics is the dual-edged sword of interconnectedness. Globalization has facilitated trade, travel, and communication, but it has also enabled the rapid spread of pathogens across borders. The Black Death spread along trade routes, the Spanish Flu was exacerbated by the movement of troops and civilians during World War I, and COVID-19 quickly became a global crisis due to international travel. This interconnectedness makes us more vulnerable to pandemics, highlighting the importance of international cooperation and coordinated responses in managing global health threats.

- **Evolution of Public Health Responses:** Over the centuries, public health responses to pandemics have evolved significantly. From early practices of quarantine and isolation during the Black Death to the development of vaccines and antibiotics in the 20th century, each pandemic has driven advancements in our understanding of disease prevention and control. The germ theory revolutionized public health, leading to improved sanitation, vaccination programs, and the establishment of public health institutions. The 21st century has seen further innovations with digital health technologies, genomic surveillance, and rapid vaccine development, exemplified by the COVID-19 response.

- **Social and Cultural Transformations:** Pandemics have also been catalysts for profound social and cultural transformations. The Black Death led to a reevaluation of religious and social norms, contributing to the decline of feudalism and the rise of a market-based economy. The HIV/AIDS epidemic transformed attitudes toward LGBTQ+ rights and health, while COVID-19 has reshaped work, education, and social interaction through digital transformation and remote engagement. These social and cultural shifts reflect the adaptability and resilience of human societies in the face of crisis.

- **Economic Disruptions and Recovery:** The economic impact of pandemics is often severe and far-reaching, affecting every sector and region of the world. The sudden economic downturns caused by pandemics can lead to widespread unemployment, business closures, and financial instability. However, these crises also present opportunities for economic innovation and resilience. The post-pandemic recoveries have often been characterized by significant technological advancements, shifts in labor markets, and new economic paradigms, as seen in the Roaring Twenties following the Spanish Flu and the digital economy boom during COVID-19.

- **Ethical and Practical Considerations:** Pandemics raise important ethical and practical considerations, particularly around equity, access to healthcare, and the balance between individual rights and public health. The disparities in vaccine access during the COVID-19 pandemic highlighted the need for a more equitable global health system. Ethical considerations also extend to the use of digital technologies for surveillance and contact tracing, which, while effective, raise concerns about privacy and data security. Addressing these ethical challenges is crucial for building trust and ensuring effective public health responses.

Reflection on Human Resilience and Adaptation

Throughout history, pandemics have challenged human societies in profound ways, testing our resilience and forcing us to adapt to new realities. Yet, time and again, humanity has demonstrated an extraordinary capacity to adapt, innovate, and overcome in the face of adversity.

- **Resilience in the Face of Crisis:** Human resilience is a recurring theme in the story of pandemics. Despite the fear, uncertainty, and loss associated with these crises, people have found ways to persevere and rebuild. During the Black Death, communities adapted to the devastating loss of life by reorganizing labor markets and agricultural practices, leading to economic and social transformation. In the wake of the Spanish Flu, societies emerged stronger, embracing technological innovation and new cultural norms that defined the Roaring Twenties.
- **Adaptation and Innovation:** Pandemics have often been catalysts for innovation. The necessity to respond to a health crisis has driven advancements in science, medicine, and technology. The development of vaccines for diseases like smallpox, polio, and COVID-19 represents significant milestones in medical science. The rapid development of mRNA vaccines for COVID-19, in particular, showcases the remarkable speed at which scientific innovation can occur when driven by urgent need. Similarly, the HIV/AIDS epidemic spurred the development of antiretroviral therapies and new approaches to community-based healthcare.
- **Community and Solidarity:** Another aspect of human resilience is the ability to come together in times of crisis. Pandemics often bring out the best in people, fostering a sense of community and solidarity. During the COVID-19 pandemic, mutual aid networks, volunteer groups, and community organizations mobilized to support those

most affected by the crisis. In cities around the world, people found creative ways to stay connected and support each other, whether through virtual gatherings, neighborhood support groups, or collective actions to protect vulnerable populations. This sense of community and solidarity has been a crucial factor in building resilience and navigating the challenges of pandemics.

- **Learning from Experience:** One of the most important aspects of human resilience is the ability to learn from past experiences and apply those lessons to future challenges. The lessons learned from past pandemics, such as the importance of early detection, rapid response, and international cooperation, have informed public health strategies and policies. The experience of COVID-19 has underscored the need for stronger global health governance, investment in public health infrastructure, and equitable access to healthcare. By learning from the past, we can better prepare for the future and build a more resilient and prepared world.

Final Thoughts on the Lessons Learned from Pandemics

The history of pandemics offers valuable lessons for the future, highlighting both the progress we have made and the challenges that remain. As we reflect on the lessons learned from past pandemics, several key takeaways emerge:

- **Preparedness is Key:** One of the most critical lessons from pandemics is the importance of preparedness. Early detection, rapid response, and effective public health measures are essential for preventing the spread of infectious diseases and mitigating their impact. Investing in public health infrastructure, surveillance systems, and research is crucial for building preparedness and resilience to future pandemics.

- **Global Cooperation is Essential:** Pandemics are inherently global challenges that require coordinated global responses. The COVID-19 pandemic has underscored the importance of international cooperation, information sharing, and collaboration in managing pandemics. Strengthening global health governance frameworks, promoting equitable access to resources, and fostering a spirit of solidarity and collaboration will be essential for future pandemic preparedness and response.

- **Equity and Inclusion Matter:** The disparities in access to healthcare, vaccines, and resources during pandemics highlight the need for a more equitable and inclusive global health system. Ensuring that all populations have access to essential healthcare services, treatments, and vaccines is not only a matter of justice but also critical for effective pandemic response. Addressing social determinants of health, promoting equity, and reducing disparities will be key to building a more resilient and inclusive global health system.

- **Adaptation and Innovation Drive Progress:** The ability to adapt and innovate has been a hallmark of human response to pandemics. Whether through the development of new vaccines, the use of digital technologies for surveillance and communication, or the reimagining of social and economic structures, innovation has been critical to navigating the challenges of pandemics. Encouraging innovation, investing in research and development, and fostering a culture of adaptability and learning will be essential for addressing future health threats.

- **The Importance of Trust and Communication:** Trust is a fundamental component of effective public health responses to pandemics. Building and maintaining trust requires transparent communication, honesty, and accountability. Public health authorities must engage with communities, provide clear and accurate information, and address concerns and misinformation. Effective communication is crucial for promoting public health measures, encouraging vaccine uptake, and fostering compliance with public health guidelines.

- **A Call to Action:** As we look to the future, the lessons learned from past pandemics should serve as a call to action. The threat of future pandemics is real and imminent, and we must be proactive in our efforts to prepare and respond. This requires a commitment to strengthening public health systems, investing in research and innovation, promoting equity and inclusion, and fostering international cooperation. By working together and learning from the past, we can build a safer, healthier, and more resilient world for all.

A Vision for the Future

The story of pandemics is not just a story of disease and death, but also a story of resilience, adaptation, and hope. It is a story that reflects the enduring human spirit to overcome adversity, learn from experience, and build a better future. As we move forward, let us carry these lessons with us, recognizing that the challenges of pandemics are not insurmountable, but rather opportunities for growth, innovation, and progress.

The future of pandemics and global health security will depend on our ability to learn from the past, act in the present, and prepare for the future. By fostering a culture of preparedness, promoting global cooperation, and embracing innovation and equity, we can build a world that is better equipped to face the challenges of pandemics and ensure the health and well-being of all people. The journey ahead may be uncertain, but with resilience, collaboration, and determination, we can create a future that is safe, healthy, and resilient for generations to come.

Appendices

Glossary of Terms

- **Antibiotic Resistance:** The ability of bacteria and other microorganisms to withstand the effects of an antibiotic that once killed them or stopped their growth. It is a growing concern in the treatment of infectious diseases, exacerbated by the overuse and misuse of antibiotics.

- **Antiretroviral Therapy (ART):** A treatment regimen for HIV/AIDS that uses a combination of drugs to suppress the virus, reduce viral load, and prevent the progression of the disease. ART has transformed HIV from a fatal illness to a manageable chronic condition.

- **Contact Tracing:** A public health strategy used to identify, assess, and manage people who have been exposed to a contagious disease to prevent further transmission. It is a key component in managing infectious disease outbreaks.

- **Digital Health:** The use of information and communication technologies (ICT) in medicine and other health professions to manage illnesses, reduce risks, and promote wellness. This includes telemedicine, mobile health apps, and electronic health records.

- **Epidemiology:** The study of how diseases spread and can be controlled in populations. It involves understanding the distribution, patterns, and determinants of health and diseases in defined populations.

- **Genomic Surveillance:** The process of sequencing the genome of pathogens to monitor and analyze their evolution, spread, and variations. It is crucial in identifying new variants and guiding public health responses to infectious diseases.

- **Global Health Security:** The activities required, both proactive and reactive, to minimize the danger and impact of acute public health events that endanger the collective health of populations globally.

- **Herd Immunity:** A form of indirect protection from infectious disease that occurs when a sufficient percentage of a population has become immune to an infection, either through vaccination or previous infections, thereby reducing the likelihood of infection for individuals who lack immunity.

- **International Health Regulations (IHR):** A legally binding framework agreed upon by WHO member states to prevent, protect against, control, and respond to the international spread of disease. The regulations are intended to enhance national, regional, and global public health security.
- **Isolation:** The separation of people who are infected with a contagious disease from those who are not infected, to prevent the spread of the disease.
- **Pandemic:** An epidemic that has spread across a large geographic area, affecting a substantial proportion of the population. Pandemics can cause significant social, economic, and health impacts.
- **Public Health:** The science and practice of protecting and improving the health of people and their communities. This includes efforts to promote healthy lifestyles, prevent diseases and injuries, and control the spread of infectious diseases.
- **Quarantine:** A public health practice used to stop or limit the spread of disease by separating and restricting the movement of people who may have been exposed to a contagious disease but are not yet symptomatic.
- **Surveillance:** The continuous, systematic collection, analysis, and interpretation of health-related data needed for planning, implementation, and evaluation of public health practice. Surveillance is essential for identifying outbreaks and guiding public health responses.
- **Vaccine:** A biological preparation that provides active acquired immunity to a particular infectious disease. Vaccines typically contain agents resembling a disease-causing microorganism and are often made from weakened or killed forms of the microbe or its toxins.

- **Vector:** An organism, such as a mosquito or tick that transmits pathogens from one host to another, spreading diseases like malaria, dengue, and Lyme disease.

Timeline of Major Pandemics

- **Plague of Athens (430 B.C.):** An unknown epidemic that struck Athens during the Peloponnesian War, killing a large portion of the population and significantly impacting the course of the war.
- **Antonine Plague (165-180 A.D.):** Likely caused by smallpox or measles, this pandemic spread throughout the Roman Empire, killing an estimated 5 million people.
- **Justinian Plague (541-542 A.D.):** Often considered the first recorded pandemic of the bubonic plague, it devastated the Byzantine Empire, killing an estimated 25-50 million people over two centuries of recurring outbreaks.
- **Black Death (1347-1351):** The most infamous pandemic in history, caused by the bubonic plague, which killed an estimated 75-200 million people across Europe, Asia, and Africa.
- **Columbian Exchange and Native American Pandemics (15th-16th Century):** The introduction of Old World diseases, such as smallpox, measles, and influenza, to the Americas following European contact decimated indigenous populations, with some estimates suggesting up to 90% mortality.
- **Great Plague of London (1665-1666):** The last major outbreak of the bubonic plague in England, which killed an estimated 100,000 people, about a quarter of London's population at the time.
- **Third Cholera Pandemic (1852-1860):** Originating in India, this pandemic spread to Asia, Europe, North America, and Africa, killing over a million people. It was the most deadly of the seven cholera pandemics.
- **Russian Flu (1889-1890):** Considered the first true modern influenza pandemic, it spread rapidly across continents due to advancements in transportation, killing an estimated 1 million people.
- **Spanish Flu (1918-1919):** The deadliest influenza pandemic in modern history, caused by the H1N1 influenza A virus, which

infected a third of the world's population and killed an estimated 50 million people.

- **HIV/AIDS Epidemic (1980s-Present):** A global pandemic that emerged in the late 20th century, caused by the human immunodeficiency virus (HIV). It has claimed over 36 million lives and remains a significant public health challenge.
- **SARS Pandemic (2002-2003):** Caused by the SARS coronavirus (SARS-CoV), it resulted in over 8,000 cases and 774 deaths worldwide, with significant economic and social impact, especially in Asia.
- **H1N1 Influenza Pandemic (2009-2010):** Also known as the "swine flu," this pandemic was caused by a novel H1N1 influenza virus, which spread globally and led to an estimated 151,700 to 575,400 deaths in the first year.
- **Ebola Outbreaks (1976, 2014-2016):** The 2014-2016 West African Ebola outbreak was the largest in history, infecting over 28,000 people and killing more than 11,000. Ebola remains a recurrent threat in some regions.
- **COVID-19 Pandemic (2019-Present):** Caused by the novel coronavirus SARS-CoV-2, COVID-19 has become one of the most widespread and impactful pandemics of the 21st century, with over 200 million cases and millions of deaths worldwide. It has caused unprecedented global social, economic, and public health disruptions.

Don't miss out!

Visit the website below and you can sign up to receive emails whenever Oswald D. B. publishes a new book. There's no charge and no obligation.

https://books2read.com/r/B-A-XWOIB-IZJYE

BOOKS2READ

Connecting independent readers to independent writers.